Preface...	5
Introduction..	7
The Early Years..................................	9
Middle School Years...........................	13
High School Years..............................	20
Freshman Year of College..................	34
The Price was Right............................	44
Undergraduate Years..........................	50
Graduate School.................................	59
Discovering Asperger's Syndrome......	79
Resolution and Some Final Thoughts..	87
References...	103
Aspie Self-Checklist...........................	104
Gray Center Information.....................	110

© 2005 Nicolas W. Dubin

Acknowledgements

This book would not have been possible without the continued support and belief my parents have displayed in me over the years. They have never given up on me even during the most trying of times.

I would like to thank some important people in my life who have always believed in me, even when I didn't. I couldn't have written the book without the support of Julia Press. She has been instrumental in helping me push forward in life. I'd like to extend a special thank you to Katie Kramer, Adrienne "Sissy" Garrison, Scot Acre, Carole Goff, Nick Thomas, Art Dubin, and Dr. John Milanovich.

To the entire faculty at the Center for Humanistic Studies as well my fellow classmates, I would like to express my gratitude for their encouragement and support.

Thank you to the tireless staff of the Gray Center for their extremely hard work and emotional support. It means the world to me. Thank you Laurel and Christy!

Editor's Note: With the exception of Dr. Milanovich, Julia Press, and Nick's parents, all other names in this book have been changed to protect the privacy of these individuals.

Preface

I have two purposes in writing this memoir of my short existence thus far on the planet: First, I want to tell you about my life as it relates to a condition called Asperger's Syndrome which is on the high end of the autism spectrum. Secondly, I would like to join notable authors such as Jerry Newport, Temple Grandin, and Stephen Shore in demystifying certain things about autism.

If you are anything like me before discovering Asperger's Syndrome, the word "autism" was probably reserved for a conversation about the movie, *RAINMAN*. The fact is there are people who are categorized as autistic who have Ph.D's in a variety of subjects. There are police officers, taxi cab drivers, artists, musicians, and individuals in careers who have autism. High functioning autism, which is frequently considered to be synonymous with Asperger's Syndrome, will be making headlines in the next few years. The fact that someone with autism could achieve a doctorate, have a professional career, write a book, or even do basic daily tasks would have seemed inconceivable a few decades ago.

But society is evolving, and with our evolution comes the knowledge that people come in all shapes and sizes. Some of us may have a variance in our neurological wiring, but we may not stick out physically upon first inspection. We may not even seem odd behaviorally upon an initial meeting, which is why Asperger's is often called a "hidden disability." More accurately stated, the hidden barriers to social communication are often present. The barriers I am referring to are invisible and intangible but nevertheless present. They are the "soft signs" that make having Asperger's Syndrome so difficult. Whereas with classic autism the barriers are visible and obvious, with Asperger's it is more subtle. As a result, other people

© 2005 Nicolas W. Dubin

may wonder why there seems to be a hidden disconnect between themselves and the individual with Asperger's. They may blame themselves for not knowing how to get close to that person, or they may blame the person with Asperger's. Truthfully though, it is nobody's fault. But make no mistake; we are extremely different from non-autistics, also referred to as neurotypicals.

There are many academic textbooks on the subject of Asperger's Syndrome. This is not one of them. This book is a memoir about my life and how it relates to Asperger's or autism. I'm assuming you, the reader, have some familiarity with Asperger's Syndrome. If you do not, perhaps it will be to your advantage to read this book before delving into any academic texts. The definitions and terminology in the academic books might make more sense once they are put into context.

Perhaps after finishing this book you will have an idea what it's like to walk in the shoes of someone with Asperger's Syndrome. Maybe, you will have a better understanding of how we look at the world.

I do not pretend to speak on behalf of the whole Asperger population. People with Asperger's syndrome are as different from one another as neurotypicals are from each other. I can only share my own life experiences in the hope this will shed some light on this often confusing subject.

I do not know your reasons for reading this book. Maybe you have a son or daughter who has been diagnosed with Asperger's, or who you suspect might have the syndrome. Maybe you yourself have it, or perhaps your spouse. Whatever the reason, I'm glad you picked up this book. I hope that it's both informative and enlightening for your purposes.

Introduction

I remember the day as if it were yesterday. In late November 1986, my parents and I were on a trip to Los Angeles to visit some family friends. I was nine years old. Our hotel was less then two miles away from Television City, where all the CBS game shows were taped.

We ate breakfast before the taping. I couldn't believe that in a few minutes, I would be sitting in the same studio where many great television programs had been and were being recorded. I was an "expert" in old television shows, especially game shows. Studio 33 was the studio where the Carol Burnett Show, the Tracy Ulman Show, The Price is Right, the $25,000 & $100,000 Pyramids, and Password were all recorded. Now, after being an avid watcher of the game show Card Sharks, I was going to actually see the show in person. It was like buying a ticket to heaven, except tickets for television shows are free, which made it even better.

For me, seeing Card Sharks was what it would be like for most nine year olds to go to Disneyland for the first time. Waiting outside on the benches to get into the studio, beat waiting in line for the Magic Mountain ride. I knew I would remember this moment all of my life.

As the usher led us to our seats, I noticed that the studio looked twenty times smaller in person than it did on television. At first, I thought that it couldn't be the same studio. Minutes later the announcer of the show, Gene Wood, came out to greet the audience and that's when I knew we were in the right spot!

I had heard Gene Wood's voice on many different game shows, and this was my chance to see what the man actually looked like. I had imitated him in my room

© 2005 Nicolas W. Dubin

countless times. "It's time for the FAAAAMILY FEUUUUUD. Introducing the Johnson family; Reg, Tina, Dan, Marla and Scott, READY FOR ACTION!" After all this time I was going to see the man in action! I couldn't believe it.

After Gene's warm-up it was time for the show to begin. The studio went dark momentarily. Then in a flash, the show began. Up to that point it was possibly the happiest 30 minutes of my life! Since that time, I have attended many other game shows, and was even a winning contestant on The Price is Right.

As a kid I knew I was different. Those differences seemed to surface more in adolescence but they were always there. My interests, for starters, were unusual, even as a third grader. Besides the intense interest in game shows I knew everything about expressways and highways. I knew that interstate 90's Eastern terminus was Boston and the Western terminus was Seattle. As a matter of fact, I could tell you the starting and ending points of any interstate highway in the country. I could even include major cities that each one passed through. People knew if they needed directions I was the guy to ask.

But it wasn't just some of my interests that alerted me to being different. It was also my way of being, my taste in music, my indifference to popular culture, and my lack of sociability, especially when puberty arrived. Only recently, at the age of 27 have I been able to put the pieces of the puzzle together and discover with the help of a neuro-psychologist, that I have Asperger's Syndrome. Had I acquired this information earlier in my life, I would have seemed like less of an enigma to myself and to others.

Chapter 1

The Early Years

I was born Nicolas Weil Dubin, on April 11, 1977 at William Beaumont Hospital in Royal Oak Michigan. My parents, Larry and Kitty, are remarkable people. Mom was a counselor for about 25 years, and she is also an acclaimed playwright. Dad has been a law professor at a Detroit area university for 30 years. He had just started teaching when I was born after practicing law for several years.

The early part of one's existence is something few people can recall, so most of what I'm about to recount is hearsay. According to my parents they began to notice something was different about me when I was around two years old. They used to take me to a city park within walking distance from our house. I loved swinging on the swings and going down the slide. However, I thought the slide was mine—literally-- that it belonged to me. Apparently, if any other children even came close to the slide when I was on it, I'd throw a huge temper tantrum. I didn't want to play with the other children. I wanted that slide entirely to myself.

At nursery school, teachers often commented that I would isolate myself and not play with other children. I also had a tendency to flap my hands up and down when I got excited, which is a trait of autism. I was in a world of my own most of the time, sometimes completely oblivious to everyone around me.

Mom and Dad also began to notice a delay in my speech. At two and a half I was barely talking. Special education professionals had recommended that my

© 2005 Nicolas W. Dubin

parents take me to a speech pathologist to address the problem. The initial diagnosis was *echolalia* (a repetition of words and phrases I had heard others use) and *aphasia* (difficulty with comprehension, as well as articulating my ideas).

The speech pathologist's office was located in the same hospital where I was born. I actually remember a few of my sessions with Cathy, when I was only three years old. She would sit with me on the floor and do various activities. Sometimes she would show me pictures of different objects and ask me to identify them. As I progressed, the activities became more challenging. I would have to turn over an object while being asked to give her another object. In other words she'd say:

"Turn over the picture of the orange, and give me the picture of the chair".

This was very difficult for me. I had a hard time remembering both directions at the same time. There were obviously some auditory processing issues taking place.

The activities really helped to sharpen my verbal acumen. Within six months, I made tremendous progress with Cathy. Instead of having a speech delay, I was now above average in terms of verbal ability. Cathy told my parents she thought I might possibly be gifted.

Still other problems were prevalent. My socialization skills were below what was expected developmentally. I rarely played with children my own age. Our next-door neighbors had four boys. Although two of them were around my age, I tended to play with the other two who were a few years younger than me. Most of the literature I've read indicate that a common Asperger trait is that we (people with Asperger's

Syndrome) have a hard time socializing with those our own age.

By first grade it was noted that I was beginning to isolate myself. This pattern of isolation continued into the following year.

In second grade there was a moment that has lived on in infamy. Perhaps it typifies so many moments I've had, some that have blended into oblivion and faded into obscurity. But this one sticks in my mind because in this moment I realized I was truly different from other kids.

I was sitting in the learning resource center (LRC), a classroom for special education students. The teacher asked Meghan and me to go to Mrs. D's second grade classroom to get two students who were late for their scheduled time in LRC. When Meghan and I got down to Mrs. D's room, I knocked on the door and was told to come in. I tried turning the handle and it seemed to stay locked.

"Mrs. D..........I can't open the door", I said.

"What do you mean you can't open the door?" she queried sarcastically.

"I can't open the door. It's stuck!"

"It's stuck? That's nonsense. Meghan, open the door, would you please?" she said.

This was a relief. I figured Meghan would fail to open the door, which would prove something was wrong with the door. But the strangest thing happened. Meghan opened the door with ease, as if she were picking up the telephone. My jaw dropped. How did that happen? Something's not wrong with the door, something must be wrong with me.

© 2005 Nicolas W. Dubin

"Now open the door young man!" demanded the teacher.

By this time I could hear the other kids laughing at my expense. Standing there with sweat dripping from my forehead I tried to pry that stubborn door open. It simply would not budge.

"Meghan", she said. "Open the door again."

Of course she did, and by this time I was completely humiliated.

"You mean to tell me that you're in second grade, and you can't even open a door? What's wrong with you?"

Those harsh words brought tears to my eyes. I ran away, disgusted and ashamed of myself, wishing there was a small hole I could crawl into.

Why couldn't I open the door? It was a door that required me to turn the knob counter-clockwise. Being characteristically rigid, I believed there was only one way to open a door. For the life of me I could not conceive that a door could be opened counter-clockwise. But other students in the second grade could reason that if a door didn't open by turning the knob one way, you should simply turn the knob the other way. I just didn't get it and I struggled publicly with this lesson in "door physics" for at least ten minutes, even though it seemed like hours.

Unfortunately, the aforementioned episode was typical of my day- to- day school experiences all the way through high school. Perhaps these episodes intensified in quantity by the time middle school arrived. It seemed as if something like this happened at least once a day, if not more. Besides embarrassing moments, there was the strain of feeling like a full-time freak.

Chapter 2

Middle School Years

From sixth grade on, my life was very unpleasant socially. I noticed that kids who were nice to me in elementary school were no longer my friends. Bullies started coming out in full force and would not relent. Most kids weren't afraid to tell me they thought I was weird, and I guess some of my behaviors didn't help matters. For a while I tried giving kids money to get them to like me. I was incredibly naïve.

I thought if I could be funny, maybe kids would like me. So I would do impersonations of televangelists, and developed a routine that became known as "the preacher." Kids would come up to me in the hallway and say,

"Dubin, do the preacher. Do the preacher."

I heard it everyday. Many times, close to fifty kids would begin gathering once word spread that I was going to do the routine.

I realize now "the preacher" was nothing more than a subconscious way of saying to other kids, "Here I am. Notice me! I don't get invited to your parties, I'm not a part of the 'in-crowd', but for a few minutes, make me feel important." And it certainly did.

My parents received a report from a counselor in middle school that I was isolating myself. The counselor recommended a therapy group for middle school aged children who were struggling socially. When Dad first presented the idea he told me that I should go and if I didn't like it I would never have to go back. I said absolutely not--I wouldn't hear of it! Me, go to a group where I knew kids were going to be different, like me?? Certainly not! But guess what? The initial request soon turned into a mandatory weekly sentence.

I hated it! I refused to participate. Sure, my parents could make me go, but they couldn't make me talk. I sat there, week after week, saying absolutely nothing. One day Dr. S wanted to meet with my parents and me to discuss my uncooperativeness during the group sessions. She told my parents to stand their ground and not be intimidated into letting me out of the group. I told her,

"You're like Saddam Hussein keeping me prisoner like this."

Dad was furious and stormed out of the office. Mom sat there mortified, while Dr. S stoically sat as if she had heard kids tell her that a million times. My strategy seemed logical to me; if I was rude enough, maybe she would let me out of the group. Unfortunately my strategy fell through. I was stuck in that group.

Finally after a couple of years, I was released from the group. My resistance to "feeling different" probably cost me a good experience in terms of connecting with other kids who had similar social struggles.

Aside from being on the basketball team for three years in middle school, I spent most of my time on the social sidelines. Mom and Dad made me go to the school dances because they knew I wouldn't go if they didn't insist. I would sit in the corner and watch the other kids enter the tumultuous period of puberty on the dance floor. Meanwhile I would stand there feeling like a total outsider.

Determined to convince a fellow student I was indeed experiencing puberty I did a pretty stupid thing. In eighth grade Dad signed me up for a special trip with a select group of eighth graders for a tour of Williamsburg, Virginia. One night in the hotel room one of my roommates was looking through an adult magazine.

"Hey Dubin, wanna buy this from me?" he asked.

"Sure, how much?"

A grin flashed upon his face as he said, "Fifteen dollars."

"Sure, I'll buy it."

As hard as this might be to believe, at the time I had no idea what a magazine like that cost. Not aware I had done anything stupid I came back to school the following Monday and word had already spread that Dubin bought this magazine for fifteen bucks. I was the laughing stock of the eighth grade, chiefly because my naïveté and gullibility got the best of me. Perhaps in my ultimate desire to fit in I caused the opposite to happen.

I haven't yet explained that I happened to be a really good tennis player. This went against logic and quite frankly was a paradox, because early diagnostic tests had indicated severe deficiencies in my fine and gross motor skills. While my fine motor skills never caught up, there must have been some serious neurological synapses when my father first handed me a tennis racquet. For reasons I haven't yet understood -- and perhaps God only knows-- I really took to the game of tennis.

It's fair to say I didn't really have any friends at the middle school I attended. I did however have friends, or at the very least, acquaintances outside of school. I always found solace in heading over to the local tennis club to take lessons when the school day ended. I knew

© 2005 Nicolas W. Dubin

the kids there would forgive my social ineptitudes because they realized I had a talent for playing tennis. Needless to say it was quite a different experience from the day-to-day doldrums of school. These kids actually respected me, and didn't tease me. They didn't see me as a freak and I felt valued there. It was then that I made up my mind to use tennis as a social vehicle. I had every intention of playing tennis in high school and figured it would be a great way to get kids to like me.

Perhaps my shining moment in middle school occurred at my Bar Mitzvah. Years later, I was told that my speech that day made an impact on the people who attended the ceremony.

Our family belonged to a secular humanistic Jewish Temple, which essentially means that the focus was on cultural Judaism as opposed to religious Judaism. The rabbi of the temple, an outspoken and original thinker, had a very unique way of conducting Bar Mitzvah's that was different from most other temples. At his synagogue the Bar Mitzvah boy was to research many Jewish heroes and select one that he felt made a positive difference in the world. Once a hero was selected, the boy or girl was to write a paper detailing life events to present to the congregation. My choice was the great vaudevillian comedian, George Burns. There was just something I liked about him. He had a warm and gentle humor. And from what I knew, he was also a humanitarian.

I spent about seven months with my tutor researching his life. I watched his movies, read his books, and finally wrote the paper.

On the day of my Bar Mitzvah I was extremely nervous. I can remember sitting in the rabbi's office before it was time for me to head into the congregation. There was sweat pouring down my face, and my heart was beating rapidly. I was sure my social awkwardness would show as I gave my speech.

Surprisingly, just the opposite occurred. I appeared more confident giving that speech than I did interacting with people on an individual basis. I thought there was something strange about this since I had heard the number one fear among Americans is public speaking. Number two is death. So obviously, the lack of the interpersonal component of giving a speech was easier for me to handle. This wouldn't become obvious to me until years later.

To be honest, the hardest part of that day for me was the reception afterwards. Interacting with the adults-- even though they were all congratulating me-- was very taxing. I can remember just wanting to get out of there.

The next day I had my party for the kids my own age. I invited my few tennis acquaintances, two good friends from Los Angeles who were friends of the family, and some kids from my middle school who I didn't even like. The reason I invited them was because I didn't want my party to have only five kids. I had been to Bar Mitzvah parties where a hundred friends were in attendance, so I certainly didn't want to give the impression to my tennis pals and out of town friends that Nick Dubin was friendless.

To my surprise many of the kids I invited from school came. However, they acted like it wasn't my party. From my own recollections as well as the videotape my dad shot of the party, none of them interacted with me. It was quite strange, because to a great extent I felt as though I was at someone else's Bar Mitzvah party, not

© 2005 Nicolas W. Dubin

my own. I remember feeling the same way the day before when I wanted to leave the reception only the feeling had greater intensity. I felt alone when I realized none of the people who came from my school were really my friends. They weren't there to celebrate the occasion of me becoming a Bar Mitzvah. They were there to play whirlyball and have fun. There was nothing wrong with them having fun and playing whirlyball, but what about me?

    I can remember the day of my middle school graduation like it was yesterday. I was feeling both grateful and scared at the same time. I was grateful that I would be leaving a school that I did not care for, but also scared that high school would be even more socially problematic than middle school.

    The graduation party was a nightmare. I felt like I was the only one there without anyone to talk to. Everyone was dancing, talking, laughing, and reminiscing except me.

    My parents obviously knew that I struggled socially in middle school. They were looking into different high schools I might be able to attend, where I could come in as the "new kid." For reasons I don't understand to this day, I refused to go anywhere except Seaholm, the high school I was supposed to attend. This was the high school where all of my middle school classmates would be going. I was stubborn as a mule.

    "But Nick, these other schools would have a much better environment. Nice kids, nice teachers, would you at least think about it?"

    "Absolutely not", I would say.

Breaking Through Hidden Barriers

Mom and I have must had this conversation at least fifty times. She would beg me to consider an alternative, but I wouldn't have any of it. I stood firm.

Chapter 3

High School Years

High school was a true paradox. I vacillated back and forth from what seemed like a prison, to a place where I felt like I belonged-- the tennis court. Yet, for all my tennis accomplishments, I did not fit in socially with the tennis team. I was the number one singles player, named captain of the team by the coach for two years, made MVP (Most Valuable Player) for two years, and named All State my senior year. In spite of these honors I still was a social outsider with the team.

Let me make one thing clear: I don't blame the team. I was on the social periphery because I simply wasn't interested in doing the things they were. I wasn't into parties, drinking, the dating scene, or the music they liked.

I preferred to play tennis and then leave, retreating back into my "shell." It had nothing to do with being socially phobic or afraid. I simply was more content on my own. Consequently, I was on the periphery. I didn't get invited to the parties, but I didn't put the vibe out that I wanted an invitation.

The coach of our team, James, was someone with whom I had a love-hate relationship. He was a great motivator, but also a tough person to please. He pushed all of his players to be the best we could be, but it came with a price. He would say things like:

"What is this sissy girl garbage I'm seeing out here? My grandmother can hit the ball harder than this!" Or:

"We're going to be playing Andover on Thursday, and you know that they're gonna be tough, you pansies!" Sometimes he could scare the living daylights out of me. No, not sometimes, most of the time. Yet in spite of this, I liked him a lot. He made me a better tennis player and did indeed push me to become the best player I could be.

I believe winning tennis matches was more important to me than for anyone else on the team. Yes it's always nice to win, but I wanted to win to be liked. I wanted to win not only to please James but to be accepted socially. I thought maybe if I won, people would excuse my social peculiarities or my hermit-like existence. If I could show them I had talent in something, it might compensate for my social weaknesses.

Yet in spite of wanting to win for social recognition, I was not willing to compromise socially. I wouldn't drink alcohol, go to parties, and participate in other activities popular with my peer group. If being liked and popular was that important to me I would have compromised a little, but I didn't. But why did winning matches mean so much to me? If I truly didn't want to socialize, why did I care whether or not people respected me for my tennis?

After years of reflection I have a plausible theory. Tennis was my great "equalizer." Had it not been for tennis I would have had a terrible social existence in high school. But because of tennis, at least I was recognized for something. I felt important in some way. I could have the best of both worlds. I didn't have to be popular but at the same time, people would know who I was.

One of the most interesting experiences of my life was in the summer of 1994. I was 17 years old at the time, and my dad had signed me up to play tennis in

© 2005 Nicolas W. Dubin

Europe for three weeks with a group of 14 other adolescents. The one requirement for this trip was that you had to be a highly ranked tennis player, which I was at the time.

As my dad and I drove to the airport, I could feel my heart sink. After about two hours of silence, Dad and I had a conversation that I remember distinctly. Out of nowhere, I blurted:

"Dad, I feel like I'm going to be losing my freedom."

"Actually it's quite the opposite Nick. This is the ultimate taste of freedom. Do you realize that you are actually going to Europe? You're gonna see the Eiffel Tower! You're going to Amsterdam and you'll see where Anne Frank lived. I wish I could have gone to Europe and played on a tennis team when I was your age! I wish I would have had the skill of playing tennis that you have."

"What if the kids make fun of me? What if I don't fit in? Then I'll be stuck alone with them for three straight weeks! That will be torture."

"They won't make fun of you and you will fit in. Trust me on this. These kids are going to see how good you are at tennis, and they're going to respect you. And you're all going for the same reason, to play tennis. So you'll have a lot in common with them."

I didn't believe my dad. I thought he was just saying that so I would leave in good spirits. Plus, if his logic was so keen, why did I not fit in with my own high school tennis team? After all, I was the number one player and everyone on that team had tennis in common.

As I was introduced to the coaches and fellow teammates with whom I would be spending the next three

Breaking Through Hidden Barriers

weeks, I told everyone right away what my ranking was to try to garner their respect.

Immediately, I noticed that most of the kids on this team were different from the kids at my high school. The majority of them came from the east coast, and I think I was the only Midwesterner. A few of the other kids were highly eccentric, and also had trouble "fitting in" at their school. This was a total revelation for me! Other kids struggling like me, socially? I couldn't believe it! And what's more, they were tennis players.

Some of the other kids even shared my interests. My roommate, for example, liked older music, like Frank Sinatra and the Beatles. At school, I couldn't find anyone who would talk to me about Frank Sinatra, but on this trip, I found someone my age who actually shared my musical interests. Fairly close to the outset of the trip, I realized that I wasn't the outsider I always believed myself to be. With this group of kids, I belonged. It was the first time in my life that I felt that way.

For three weeks, we traveled by train to four countries and played in tournaments practically every day. We went to France, Belgium, Holland and Germany. I must admit there were times on this trip where I simply did not fit in. "Karaoke night" in Antwerp, Belgium was one of those times. Since drinking alcohol is legal for minors in Europe, the coaches of our group allowed the team to drink. This made me feel highly uncomfortable. I was angry at the coaches for being "irresponsible;" I knew they were breaking the rules established by the director of the program and using incredibly bad judgment. Although I was tempted to report the coaches to the director, I didn't. But it wasn't just the drinking that bothered me. It was the noise, smoke, and rowdiness in that Karaoke bar. I couldn't wait to leave.

Other noisy parties caused difficulty for me. I needed more downtime than I was afforded.

I also was by any kind of unpredictability. The trip was highly structured with a written itinerary for each day. I followed these almost religiously. I always needed to know what was going to happen next. Yet when something unexpected came up, it threw me into a tizzy. For example, the Karaoke Bar was not on our itinerary. It was something the coaches decided upon at the last minute. That literally freaked me out. I would have wanted some psychological time to "charge my battery" for such an occasion, and this was spur of the moment. I felt angry at the coaches and I'm sure my bitterness became obvious.

The highlight of this trip took place in the Netherlands. Our group played in a 64 person tournament. This meant it was possible for two people on our team to play against each other. I made it to the finals, winning five consecutive matches to get there. In the finals, my worst fear came true. I had to compete against one of my team members, who was regarded as the best player on the team.

That day, I played the best match of my life. I won the tournament! Immediately, I called my parents and told them the news! They were ecstatic.

Though the trip was not perfect and certainly had very hard moments for me to endure, I think it was a good decision to go. As I said before, it put me with a group of people that I shared a "special interest" with. That alone helped tremendously. Consequently, I truly felt like I belonged with this group, even though I preferred my private time more than others on the team.

Back at school however, it was an entirely different story.

By this time my social life was very restricted. I basically went to school, and went home after school. I found the lunch hour to be one of the toughest parts of the school day. Once I became an upperclassman (during the last two years of high school), I sometimes went home at lunch. Freshman and sophomore students (those in the first two years of high school) weren't allowed to leave the school during lunch hour. I went to the library and sat by myself. Most of the time, I didn't even eat lunch. I just couldn't stand being in the lunchroom seeing everyone having fun. I resented them. Why did I always have to be the one left out?

I felt that if I went to the lunchroom, people would notice that I was isolated. I was very self-conscious of others thinking I had no friends. So, in order to protect a false image, I retreated. The library was my refuge for the first two years of high school, and home was my safe haven the last two years. Obviously, coming home every day for lunch was a huge concern for my parents. Eventually I would go to a fast food restaurant in order to avoid a confrontation with my parents.

During high school I became very interested in radio. I knew everything there was to know about each radio station in Detroit. At that time I wanted to be an on-air radio disc jockey. In elementary school I had written letters to four or five major radio personalities in Detroit, all of whom invited me to come and watch them in action. I was mesmerized by the fluidity they possessed and I wanted to emulate them. In retrospect, I think my desire

© 2005 Nicolas W. Dubin

to be in radio was to compensate for my social ineptness in a public venue. In other words, this would be my way of saying to everyone, "Hey, wait a minute! I'm not socially inept! Listen to me; I'm not afraid of talking to a mass audience."

My high school offered a radio speech class which I decided to take my sophomore year. This was a prerequisite class in order to do the "school announcement," -- a class only offered to juniors and seniors.

The purpose of this broadcasting class was to produce a five minute daily show for the morning announcements. We had to create a "spot" which was really a commercial for an upcoming school event like a football game or the prom. Each person had an assigned role. There was an engineer, a director, two announcers, and the remaining people would make the daily spot.

There was a debate going on as to whether I should take the broadcasting class. In the radio speech class, I struggled greatly with something called the "reel to reel" machine, a device used to record the daily spots. My fine motor skills made it difficult for me to operate the machine correctly. After much deliberation, the broadcasting teacher finally decided that she would accept me on a trial basis. However, because I was a special education student it was written into my IEP (individual educational plan) that if needed, someone could help me with the reel to reel. I wanted to be able to operate the machine by myself but for two years I always had to ask for help. This was highly embarrassing for me.

The type of music I liked also made me stick out a little bit. The engineer got to select the music that he or she wanted to be played for the show that day. Most people would select groups like Pearl Jam, Green Day, and other alternative or heavy metal music. I on the other hand, preferred Frank Sinatra, Louis Armstrong, and the like. One day I decided to play a song by Louis Armstrong and Louis Jordan called "I'll be Glad When You're Dead, You Rascal You." I thought it was a fun, upbeat song.

After class, the teacher said nothing to me. The next day, she came up to me and said:

"Do you know that at least five teachers approached me yesterday, complaining about the lyrics of the song you choose."

Oh, no," I thought to myself.

"How could you play a song like that, and not ask me about it, when the lyrics are clearly about people killing each other? I'm going to suspend you from the announcements for two weeks."

Ultimately, I was suspended from school for a week.

Clearly what I had done was inappropriate, but I was totally oblivious.

One thing I liked about the broadcasting class was it was one more way for people to recognize me. I had accepted the fact that I was never going to be a social butterfly but I wanted to make my name known. So I had a characteristic greeting as the announcer: "Goooooooooooooooood morning Seaholm," (reminiscent of Robin William's, "Goooooooooooooooooood morning Vietnam.")

The combination of both tennis and the broadcasting class ensured that by my junior year most everyone in the school knew who I was.

During my junior year, I took a social psychology class. One day, the instructor had us do an activity that would end up completely devastating me. She had students take out sheets of paper and write down what we thought of everybody else in the class. We had to write a few adjectives describing each person.

When the papers were collected, we had an opportunity to read everyone else's comments about ourselves. I'll never forget the first one I read about myself:

"Kind of weird. Different."

The next one read:

"Strange. Really strange."

The next one:

"Weird. Paces back and forth, a lot."

Most of the comments had something to do with me being weird, strange or different. It was then that I got confirmation from the outside world that my thoughts about myself weren't crazy. I was indeed perceived as weird or strange by others. While this was somewhat of a relief confirming my sanity, it was hard for me to take. It meant I had to surrender to the idea that I was always going to walk to the beat of my own drummer. It meant I had to accept the fact that I was different. Yet, I wouldn't specifically know how I was different until the age of 27.

In retrospect, as an Aspie (having Asperger's) adult I can see why certain things about high school were challenging for me. It now makes sense that home-schooling is a plausible alternative for some Aspie teenagers.

One thing that was very difficult about high school was that I was constantly feeling over stimulated by my environment. There was so much to process, and learning new information was taxing due to my slow processing speeds. I learn information very slowly, as do a lot of people with Asperger's Syndrome. It takes me longer to process information than the average person. As a result, when everyone was moving onto the next concept, I was usually stuck on the one before it. Once I finally "got it", I was exhausted because it took that much more energy.

Also, attempts at socializing were difficult due to a feeling of complete inadequacy in the social arena. Consequently, socializing required lots of energy. During the course of a day in high school you might see fifty people that you know. You may not necessarily be friends with all those people, but you may have to interact with them in some superficial, congenial way. Every interaction was a challenge for me in some way or another. Whether it was responding to a quick joke, commenting about something trivial, or remembering someone's name, it was extremely difficult. I struggle no less with these issues today, but now understand that the difficulties I have are not my fault.

Every year there was one particular day that was completely over stimulating for me and unfortunately it was a mandatory school activity. Field Day, a "school spirit day" was a day where each class (freshman, sophomore, junior & senior) competed against each other to see who had the most school spirit. There was always a panel of judges and most parents would attend this event. Each class would enter the gym doing some sort of a dance, then sing a class song, followed by the performance of a class skit.

In my opinion, field day was a loud, obnoxious, and completely unnecessary activity. It taxed me to such an extent that by the time it was over, I felt like I could sleep as long as the fabled Rip Van Winkle, who slept for

© 2005 Nicolas W. Dubin

twenty years. The gym was a cacophony of noise, the social interaction would always take me by surprise, and it was an all around tiring event.

Even as an adult, I find that there are things which fatigue me on a daily basis. Most involve over stimulation, in other words, an assault on my sensory modalities. For example, if I go to a movie my auditory and visual modalities get tired by the incoming onslaught of stimuli. This means activities that require my senses to do a lot of work tire me out. Even something as simple as going to a movie can "wipe me out". In documented literature, it is stated this is particularly true among Aspies; they can become over stimulated quite easily.

In high school, I took very few academically challenging courses. I took pre-algebra my freshman year—something I should have completed successfully in middle school.

Many of my classes were taught by special education teachers in an individualized setting. By the time I got around to taking regular algebra, it was in a special education room. Ironically, I received worse grades in my special education classes than I did in my mainstream classes.

Mrs. Z was my algebra teacher. She prided herself on being called "foxy". In fact, she required students in her class to call her "Foxy Mrs. Z." I never understood it, but one day it went over the line.

On one of our tests, she had as a true/false question: "True or False: Mrs. Z is foxy."

I thought that was an outrageous question to put on a test so I marked false. As far as I was concerned, everyone would mark false and be as offended by that question as I was. That was not to be.

The next day our tests were returned and I noticed on the top of the page that I received an E. I looked to see what I got wrong, and I saw " -4," meaning I got four wrong. One of the questions marked wrong was my answer to the true/false question but that shouldn't have meant that I failed the test. There were 15 questions on the test and I missed four, so I was confused how that resulted in an E grade.

"Mrs. Z," I said.

"What?" she replied hastily.

"Um, I noticed that I only got four wrong, and I got an E on the test."

"Yeah", she said, as if I was just stating a fact.

"Well, should I have gotten an E?" I asked.

"Yeah, you didn't play the game," she said.

Game? What was she talking about?

"What game?" I asked.

"The game of life! You need to learn how to play the game of life."

At this point, I was totally lost. I had no idea what she was talking about.

"What"?

"Play the game of life," she repeated again. "You were the only person in the class to mark false on that question. Sometimes in life if you don't play the game you get in trouble. If you argue with an officer you're not playing the game and guess what, he can arrest you. So this is a life lesson I'm teaching you."

Even at the young and naïve age of 17, I knew what she was doing was completely inappropriate. So I went to my case manager, Mrs. C and explained the circumstances. Mrs. C was the director of special education at Seaholm and she was an interim director.

© 2005 Nicolas W. Dubin

Being an interim director, she sort of had to "play the game" or else she could have been easily let go. But guess what? Mrs. C didn't play the game. She sided with me. Mrs. C told me she was going to Mrs. Z to deal with the situation.

The next day as I entered the classroom, I saw that Mrs. Z was crying. I thought maybe someone in her family had died. I asked her if she was okay and she said nothing.

"Kids," Mrs. Z said with tears streaming down her face. "I have learned that for whatever reason, I can no longer have you call me foxy." And that was all she said.

I couldn't believe it! This is why she was crying?? Was she doing this to punish me, trying to make me feel guilty for what I had done? Or was she really this crushed by being reprimanded by her supervisor as a result of one of her students? Maybe she was crushed that her class identity of being "foxy" was being stripped from her. I don't think I'll ever know.

One thing I learned from elementary and middle school was that my fine motor skills lagged far behind others. By the time I got to Seaholm, I would make a concerted effort not to take classes that required extensive use of fine motor skills. Sometimes I didn't have a choice. Ceramics for example, was a required class and I struggled to pull off a D.

There was a freshman science class I took that had an engineering component. I can't remember the specifics of what was required, but I do remember it involved a tremendous amount of attention to visual detail and the use of fine motor skills. Needless to say, I struggled mightily to get through this section of the class.

Breaking Through Hidden Barriers

Life would not change for me socially between my freshman and senior years of high school. I took very few social risks, did not date at all and preferred keeping to myself.

Chapter 4

Freshman Year of College

I graduated from Seaholm High School with a G.P.A (Grade Point Average) around a 2.7 (out of a possible 4.0). Though most of my grades were mediocre, there were always some classes that would manage to pull up my G.P.A. Broadcasting was a class I could usually count on for an A, along with classes like T.V production. I felt fairly happy that I was able to graduate from high school with a "B-average" even though I admit I put little effort into my academic coursework in high school.

From the time I entered high school, there was never a doubt in my mind that I would go to college. I went to a high school where almost 95% of the students were college bound so the academic standards were quite high. Most students who didn't go to college either "flunked out" or dropped out. Those who graduated from Seaholm usually ended up pursuing higher education.

But something about college really and truly scared me. I knew that if I didn't start socializing I might become a recluse as an adult. I was also cognizant of how socially inept I was and frankly, how much I hated to socialize. So this was my biggest challenge.

This challenge is what inspired me to go away my freshman year instead of staying home and commuting. I knew deep down if I stayed at home, there was a greater chance I would remain in my snuggly comfort zone. I also thought there was a hidden expectation among people who attended Seaholm to go away and not stay home.

Breaking Through Hidden Barriers

As it turns out, this was truly just my own perception. I was afraid of being thought of as "uncool" if I stayed home and commuted. There were obviously conflicting forces at work in terms of my decision to go away; one force was reasonable, the other was irrational.

So I headed to Grand Valley State University, more than 150 miles from home.

Throughout the summer of 1996, I questioned my decision over and over again. I had already been accepted and there was no turning back. Somehow an inner voice seemed to tell me, "You're not ready." My parents were very encouraging and tried to prepare me emotionally to "leave the nest," but I didn't feel ready. It wasn't that I didn't feel ready academically. Socializing is what made me the most anxious.

The major difference between high school and college was that I wouldn't have my parents at my beck and call. They wouldn't be in the next room, ready to console me after an upsetting day. They wouldn't be there to spend time with me on weekends, and be my only true friends. No, at Grand Valley I would be without them. This was a terrible thought for me to consider, and I was terrified every time I thought about it.

I vividly remember the day my parents drove me up to school. I was teary-eyed the whole two and a half hour drive. It felt weird and wrong that I was going to be without my parents. They were my world, and I just couldn't live without them. Yet I would have to. They were going to drop me off and I wouldn't see them for long stretches at a time.

When we got there many people were gathered in the lobby of the dorm. I heard loud music coming from a dorm room down the hall. To my standards it seemed like

© 2005 Nicolas W. Dubin

a jungle. I looked at my parents and they knew exactly what I was thinking.

"It'll be all right Nick," said Dad. "Just hang in there."

We proceeded down the hall to find my dorm room. My new roommate, Eli, was watching television. I had spoken to him on the phone because my parents suggested this might be a good way to make a connection before meeting him. Once we got to the room, I tried being friendly.

"Hi Eli", I said.

"Hey", he said.

"What's goin' on?" I asked politely.

"Nothing, I gotta get going."

I looked at dad once again.

"Don't start taking everything personally. He probably had to go buy books."

Okay, fair enough. After all, I couldn't judge a person based upon one interaction. We stayed in the room long enough for Eli to return.

"Hey Eli", I said. "These are my parents, Kitty and Larry."

"Hi," he said politely enough.

We all chatted for a few minutes before my parents directed me outside the dorm to say their official "good-bye". I remember this as if it were yesterday.

"Mom, Dad, please don't go," I said. "I don't know if I can do this."

"Nick," Dad said. "It's already done, you're here, you have to make the most of it. I have faith in you."

And with that and a couple of teary-eyed goodbye kisses,

I was on my own. My heart sank--I was absolutely petrified.

My most immediate "emergency" was that I had a roommate! The unpredictability of it all was overwhelming: people coming in and out without warning; not giving me time to prepare; constant breaks in routine, and not being able to do things exactly when and where I wanted to. Above all there was a lack of privacy!! I valued privacy like a Buddhist Monk.

Everything about having a roommate seemed negative to me, and I'm sure I gave off a vibe of feeling very uncomfortable around Eli. Truth be told, I was. It was probably a combination of being an only child and having those hidden barriers to socialization and communication.

It didn't take long for Eli to get on my bad side. He would come in and out of the room in the middle of the night; sometimes leaving at 1:00 a.m. and coming back briefly an hour later, only to leave again. Each time he did this, it threw me into a state of disequilibrium. The door would open and clang shut several times each night, sounding like a cannon. He played loud music, totally disturbing my senses. And on top everything, he acted as if I didn't exist. He hardly ever talked to me. Whether this was because he sensed my discomfort or genuinely didn't like me, I still don't know. What I did know was that it was an intolerable situation.

About a month into the school year I met my parents at a resort about an hour away. We were joined by family friends from Chicago.

I was miserable the entire weekend and I didn't do a very good job of hiding that misery from our friends. On Sunday, Dad and I had lunch alone at a restaurant.

"Dad," I said. "I can't go on living in that dorm. I'm

© 2005 Nicolas W. Dubin

miserable.

"Okay", he said. "We'll figure something out."

My parents have always been there for me, and this was no exception. We drove back to my college that day to look for a possible rooming alternative. All the apartments in the small town of Allendale were too expensive but they knew as well as I did the situation in the dorm was mentally breaking me down. We needed a solution, and fast.

"Nick, we couldn't find anything workable today, but we're gonna keep trying," said Dad. "We'll see what else we can find. You keep looking, too and hopefully we'll be able to come up with something."

So back to the dorm I went, hoping that somehow a solution would be forthcoming. A few days later I got a call from Dad saying that somehow he was able to find a rooming house about two miles away from campus where the rent would be fairly inexpensive. I would be living with a family in their home, having a room to myself. Of course it didn't sound like an ideal situation, but anything seemed better than staying in the dorm.

That weekend Mom and Dad drove up to check out the rooming house with me. The family had three children. The father was a builder and the mother was a stay at home parent.

In order to get to my bedroom you had to enter through the family room. I tried at all costs to enter the house when I didn't think the family was going to be in the family room. Sometimes it was unavoidable. I would see them, cordially say hi, and go to my room. I interacted with them minimally.

Often times if my classes finished in the early afternoon, I wouldn't want to go back to their house.

Instead I would go for long rides in my car. Mostly I would go into the city of Grand Rapids, about twenty five minutes away from campus. I'd ride around in my car and just pass the time.

I wanted to give the family I was living with the impression that I had a life, because if I always came home after class, it would show that I didn't. I also didn't want to interact with them, and driving around aimlessly was a better alternative. It's amazing the measures I took to avoid socializing.

The fear I had about being without my parents was also coming to fruition. I was incredibly homesick and simply missed being with them. From the very first weekend until the end of the first semester, I came home every Friday, even though my college was 200 miles away. I was regularly commuting 400 miles every weekend.

If something happened which didn't permit me to come home, it would throw me into a state of pandemonium. If I didn't leave campus by 3:00 p.m. on Friday I would panic. I remember one time my car broke down on a Friday and I pleaded with the mechanic to fix it. In fact I paid him extra so that he would fix it faster.

On the drives home, I would always play the same music. In some ways, hearing the same tunes every Friday signified a freedom I felt whenever I left school. I came to call it "The hymn of freedom."

Whether there was rain, sunshine, or snow I headed home every Friday. Once winter rolled around, Michigan weather started turning nasty. One weekend we received over two feet of snow. I remember driving through some scary weather; blinding snow caused low visibility. Icy roads forced me to drive below ten miles per hour on the freeway. But it didn't matter to me. I was willing to drive through anything to see my parents on the weekends. I risked my life by driving on roads where any sane person would have stayed home with some hot chocolate, next to a cozy fire.

Positive things were happening as well. Much to everyone's surprise, I was starting to do well academically. More importantly, I was actually putting some effort into my work. My writing significantly improved my freshman year along with my general study skills. I made use of tutors in the academic skills center who assisted me greatly in getting good grades in difficult classes.

I took Ethics, taught by a Calvinist. I never knew I was so interested in the existential matters of the universe before taking this class. It opened my eyes to a whole world of thought that I had never before been exposed to. The class helped me become more introspective than I already was and it stretched my mind to think about new ideas and concepts.

When I was searching for colleges, one of the things that had attracted me to Grand Valley State University was that it seemed I would be able to join their tennis team. I had met with the coach of the men's team before being officially admitted. He said that based upon my high school record and seeing me play, he thought I could be one of the better players on the team. Grand Valley State was a division two school, which meant the school played against fairly advanced big teams. The other colleges I considered were division three schools where I would clearly make the team, or division one schools where I would be lucky to make the team as a walk-on.

Official practices began in January. Our coach was not a very good coach. He was the opposite of my high school coach, whose practices were very structured, and who demanded total respect. Somehow I managed to become the number one singles player, something I certainly wasn't expecting to do as a freshman at a division two school. I was shocked that in spite of my mental state of confusion and unhappiness, I still managed to summon up the chutzpah and energy necessary to win all my challenge matches.

The tremendous pressure I was putting on myself to win these matches made tennis quite unbearable for me. When Dad came to watch me play I would come close to vomiting before each match. He could see that the pressure of winning was getting the best of me.

Tennis posed other challenges for me. For starters, it meant that beginning late February, I could no longer go home every weekend. Often times we would have "away matches," traveling as far as Pennsylvania or the Upper Peninsula of Michigan. This was extremely difficult for me considering the fact that before this I had gone home almost 25 weekends in a row. Although it was gut-wrenching for me, it was one of the requirements of being on the team.

Predictably, socializing with the team outside of practice and matches was a huge challenge for me. During the early part of the season we had a team trip to Hilton Head, South Carolina. During the fourteen hour drive, I was crammed in a crowded van with a group of loud guys. I had no interest in their topics of discussion.

Once we arrived at Hilton Head, all I could think about was how much longer it would be before heading back home. The socializing aspect of this trip was extremely difficult. At night, the guys on the team headed to the bar and I was usually the self-imposed odd-man-out. I would choose to stay behind in the room while everyone else was having a good time.

    The place where we stayed was a noisy and busy hotel. Loud music was playing everywhere and people were yelling and screaming into all hours of the night. It was a nightmarish experience for me. I just wanted to go home--not back to college, but back home to Detroit. For me, it just couldn't come soon enough.

    As one might imagine, I did not do very well on this trip tennis-wise. I lost all three of my singles matches and did not win a doubles match either. I was clearly dejected. The coach was considering moving me to a lower position in the singles lineup. I begged him not to, so he agreed to try me out for a couple more matches at Number One. I was relieved.

    I never thought I could be even somewhat happy to be in the confines of my rooming house, but upon my return from Hilton Head, I was thrilled.

    As the season wore on, I managed to improve my singles record. On one occasion, I won the deciding match for our team. Everyone had finished but I was struggling with my match. Down a set, and 4-1, it looked as if the match was over. Somehow during the course of the set I managed to rattle my opponent by sneaking out a few breaks of serve. He was a senior well aware of my freshman status who didn't feel like I should have taken even a game off him. When I stole the second set from him he was visibly upset. From then on, I managed to keep my concentration and win the final set 6-2 which clinched the win for our team.

Back at Grand Valley I was named "athlete of the week" for the entire school. Coach was interviewed on PBS TV in Western Michigan, and described in detail the way I snuck out the win. I taped the interview from my room and was quite proud of myself, as were my parents when I showed them the interview.

Finally, late April rolled around and it was time for the GLIAC (Great Lakes) tournament conference. All the schools we had previously competed against during the season were to participate in this tournament held in Midland, Michigan. The drive to Midland from Grand Rapids is a little over two hours and as I made my way to Midland I couldn't help but feel grateful that when I left Midland I would be heading home to Detroit and not back to college.

I won my first two matches but in the third round, I lost 7-6 in a third set tiebreak to someone I had beaten previously in the season. A loss like this would have devastated me 99% of the time, but it didn't this time. Simply put, the happiness of being done with the school year outweighed any pain I was feeling about losing the match.

At long last I had completed my freshman year, and it seemed like a miracle. But soon I was to discover that the real miracle was just around the corner.

© 2005 Nicolas W. Dubin

Chapter 5

The Price was Right

Early in my freshman year Dad had made a solemn pledge to me. He said that if I could make it through the year, alive and in one piece, he would take me to Los Angeles to see a taping of *The Price is Right*. As crazy as this may sound, part of the impetus which kept me going that year was the knowledge that I would get to see my favorite game show.

In the fall of 1996, eight months from the taping, I came up with a strategy to become a contestant. As I watched the show over the years, I had noticed many contestants who got picked from the audience were those who wore special shirts with original text or a picture about The Price is Right. Shirts like, "I love Bob" or, "I want to be a Barker's Beauty" were typically chosen. So I decided to make a shirt I was sure no other contestant in the history of the show had ever worn.

As a kid I had written Bob Barker a fan letter, and had received a picture of the host. I plastered that old picture onto a sweatshirt. I decided to include some of his idiosyncratic sayings, which audiences wouldn't know unless they paid extremely close attention. The text on my shirt was as follows:

My Favorite Barker Quotes:
1. What is it about me Samoans can't resist picking me up?
2. Don't stop the range finder until you're sure of the price, because we can't start it again for 41 hours.

3. We'll have another pricing game after we have this announcement.
4. We want to see the next item up for bids fellers.
5. Bob Barker reminding you to help control the pet population, have your pet spayed or neutered.

I was sure this shirt would land me on the show.

Dad and I flew to Los Angeles from Detroit the day after I came back from Midland. I had already gotten over the disappointment of losing that tough three set match and my mind was fully concentrated on one goal-- becoming a contestant.

We decided to fly into Los Angeles and attend a taping the following day. That night as we checked into the hotel I could feel my adrenaline pumping. Just three days earlier I had been in Allendale, Michigan, a place associated with unpleasant memories. Now I was with my dad in Hollywood, California to see my favorite television show. I think I was more excited for this taping at age 20 than I was when I saw Card Sharks, exactly ten years earlier.

We arrived at Television City around 8:00 a.m. for the 4:45 p.m. taping. We sat on the same benches that I had sat on ten years previously for Card Sharks. By 3:00 p.m., my dad's patience was wearing thin.

"Nothing is worth this long of a wait," he said.

Around 3:30, two studio producers came out and sat in their director's chairs. We were told that everyone was going to be interviewed for thirty seconds, allowing them to get a feel for who would make the most energetic and fun contestants. In other words, we were being screened. Normally I would have been nervous for something like this. After all, I got nervous just being

© 2005 Nicolas W. Dubin

around the family I lived with at school for an entire year. But I had too much adrenaline rushing through me to feel nervous.

When it was my turn, I told them what a fan I was of the show and that my dad and I had come all the way from Michigan just to see The Price is Right. I'm sure they also took notice of my sweatshirt. We proceeded into the studio. Since Dad and I arrived early in the morning we were escorted to our front row seats. Two feet in front of me was the set of The Price is Right, a game show I had been watching since I was "knee high to a grasshopper." It was like being in the Land of Oz, a surreal atmosphere. I turned to Dad,

"Do you think I'm gonna get picked as a contestant?" I asked.

"We'll know pretty soon," he said.

As he would later admit, he thought I had no chance of being called to "C'mon Down!"

Rod Roddy, the announcer, came out moments later to warm up the anxiously awaiting crowd. All I could think of was what it would be like if my name was called. What would I do? How would I act? Would I win? Lose? Maybe drive away with a new car? I had a whole bunch of fantasies playing out in my head.

"Two minutes", a voice from the side of the stage called out.

My heart was pounding rapidly. The moment of truth was literally seconds away.

Finally the showed started, and Rod Roddy proceeded to say the following:

"Here it comes! Television's most exciting hour of fantastic prices! Celebrating its 25th year on CBS, the fabulous 60 minute, Price is Right! Jeff Tanner, c'mon

Breaking Through Hidden Barriers

down. Anne Burns, c'mon down. Nicolas Dubin, c'mon down."

At that moment I had no time to think. I had no time to second guess myself. I stood up and ran as fast as I could to a podium. Seconds later:

"And now, here is the star of the Price is Right, BOB BARKER!"

Was this actually happening? I had no time to think. The first item, a set of golf clubs, was immediately shown and I had to think fast in terms of coming up with a bid. I guess I can blame it on the fact I don't play golf, because I didn't even come close to guessing it right. Someone else did. He got on stage and won himself a car. Shucks!

The next item was a recycling cabinet. Anyone ever hear of a recycling cabinet? Neither had I.

The first bid was $765. Since I was the last person to bid I waited very patiently to hear what everyone else bid. The next highest bid from $765 was $1,000, so I strategically decided to bid $766. The actual retail price: $960. The winner, Nicolas!

I actually did it! I made it on stage with Bob Barker! I was hysterical, but did a good job of acting cool.

Bob led me to the center of the stage where the giant price tag was. As I stood next to him, I felt like I was standing next to my idol in the flesh. My whole trip to California was worth just that.

Bob then took notice of my shirt. He began reading the quotations one by one and as he was doing this he was trying hard not to crack up. He was visibly amused by them. When he finished reading them, he said:

"This man! I don't know myself the prizes we give

away beforehand, but you deserve something nice. I like that! Obviously you're a loyal friend and true, you watch the show, you deserve something nice; Rod, what do we have for him?"

"Something really nice--a chance to win $10,000 cash!"

Those were the sweetest words I had heard all year long.

The object of the game was to guess whether the prices of the items shown were higher or lower than the price shown. For example, if they showed a hairdryer with a price of $40, I would have to say whether the price was higher or lower than the stated price. I had to guess on a series of four items. I didn't know any of the prices but fortunately the audience did. I got all four items correct, which meant I had four opportunities to punch the board.

Behind each hole was a slip of paper indicating the amount of money I had won. The amount ranged from $50 to $10,000. Most of the board was filled with $50 slips, and the higher the numerical denomination, the fewer the slips on the board. There were only two $10,000 prizes, and less than a handful of $5,000 slips on the whole board.

My first punch was fairly successful as I accumulated $1000.

"You know," said Bob. "You could…….There's room down here (on your shirt) for a fifth quote. And my fifth quote that you might like could be; 'Nicolas you've won 1,000 dollars. Spend it wisely' And that would be the end of it."

I thought about it for maybe two seconds and replied quickly,

"As much as I'd like to put that on I think I'm going to keep going."

So he continued to check what the amount of the next hole was worth. Risking my thousand I could have easily ended up with $50 but instead, I got another thousand. At this point I had a serious choice to make. I could feel lucky that I got a thousand dollars twice and leave happy. On the other hand, I felt like something good was about to happen. It was just a feeling of intuition. I decided to keep going. Bob took a peek inside the hole, reached for the slip, and said with a grin on his face:

"Ohhhhh, Nicolas……..He had a chance for a thousand dollars, right? And then he gave it up. Then he had another chance for a thousand dollars. And he gave that up. And here he has for his consideration, $5,000!!"

I started jumping up and down, the way I did as a kid. I was so excited I could hardly contain myself. Not only was I standing next to a man I revered but I had just won $5,000 on a game show!

We got back to the hotel and called Mom to tell her the news. She was speechless.

"I can't believe it," she said. "You actually did it."

I couldn't believe it either. The impossible mission has been accomplished!

© 2005 Nicolas W. Dubin

Chapter 6

Undergraduate Years

Although I was feeling victorious from my win on The Price is Right, I suddenly had to face the reality of heading back to Grand Valley. For me, that was not a pleasant thought to contemplate. I had been feeling suicidal at times throughout my first year of college, and knew if I went back, it might push me over the edge. Without the help of a very good friend who I would meet that summer, I might have made a fatal decision.

Mom and Dad told me that during the year they had been introduced to a "spiritual" friend, whom they had met through another friend. Julia lived in New Hampshire. A friend to people around the world, she selflessly gives her time to counsel those who need and desire a spiritual friend. She asks nothing in return, including money. I had never heard of such selfless altruism in my life before Julia.

My parents saw how much I was struggling with the decision to go back to Grand Valley, and they knew we needed some outside help. Julia was going to be in town at the beginning of July so Mom arranged a family meeting with her.

I was not aware that Julia already had a good idea of who I was before she even met me. My parents had been talking to her on the phone weekly, and she had seen me on The Price is Right. She was told about my social struggles in childhood and my enduring hardships at Grand Valley. When I met Julia it was like meeting someone I had known all my life. I knew immediately that I could trust her and that she was someone with whom I would want to stay in contact.

Since Julia knew about my situation at Grand Valley, it saved a lot of explaining. I basically felt that coming home would be a defeatist move on my part but on the other hand, I also feared for my life if I went back there.

She gently said, "Nick, you have a right and responsibility to take care of yourself. You need to do what's right for you. You will still be earning a college degree, no matter what institution you go to, and that's saying a lot right there."

I had never heard it put that simply. She was right. I was worrying too much about what others would think of me. In my mind leaving Grand Valley would have been a defeatist move, but in reality I was doing what was right for me. After that meeting I was confident in my decision that I would go to school in or around Detroit.

The other difficult factor about deciding to come home was that I was probably going to give up playing tennis for a college team. On top of feeling like I couldn't survive on my own, I was worried about feeling like a failure for not playing four years of college tennis and meeting everyone's expectations.

I had noticed during my year at Grand Valley that tennis wasn't giving me the joy and gratification I expected. Even though I played number one singles and had a good year by most peoples' standards, the pressure of winning ultimately got to me. I did not have a strong bond with the team (probably in part due to my own actions) and it felt like playing competitive tennis was no longer important. Going into my sophomore year I decided to go into tennis retirement.

© 2005 Nicolas W. Dubin

And that's exactly what I did. I made the decision to come home for the beginning of my sophomore year of college.

Upon searching several in-town universities I decided to go to Oakland University, which was about fifteen minutes from where I lived. One of the schools I looked at had a tennis team but was located in the inner-city of Detroit, which was not a place I cared to drive to every day.

Oakland University was where I would ultimately obtain my bachelors degree. During my three year stint I was directionally lost in terms of a future career. My major at the time was communications, because at that point, I still thought I would be a prominent radio disc jockey.

My parents encouraged me to look into the school radio station. It seemed like a good opportunity for me to get some on-air experience to use on a future resume. I made my audition tape with the help of a technician I hired and was subsequently given an hour slot on a weekly basis.

My audition tape was completely scripted. I meticulously crafted a script that would give the history of each artist I played. I wanted to sound knowledgeable. At the time however, I had no knowledge of the music I used for that tape; I was merely copying information I read from a book. Let me explain:

After attending an orientation meeting for the radio station, one of the things I learned was that the DJ's had to play what they called "non-commercial" music. This essentially means the music is "underground", not music on the pop charts. In a way, this fit me perfectly because I despised popular music. But there wasn't one kind of music at the time that I was completely knowledgeable about. I knew I liked jazz the few times I had heard it but I didn't know much about it. So when I made my audition tape I was acting like I was an expert on jazz, when I really wasn't.

But somehow through the grace of a higher power perhaps, I was slotted an hour. The problem was I felt I had to become an expert. Anything less would make me feel publicly stupid, which was unacceptable to me. So I went on a buying rampage of every jazz album I could find. Where did I get the money? You guessed it, The Price is Right. I used the money I accumulated on The Price is Right to build up an extensive jazz collection. I had to know my music thoroughly before playing it on the air.

As I became an expert on the subject of jazz, I started to fall in love with the music. I couldn't get enough jazz. It sort of became like an addiction to me. I had to have it playing everywhere; in my car, at home, even in my walkman as I traveled around campus. I couldn't believe that for twenty-one years, I lived without this music in my life. It was clear throughout my undergraduate years, jazz would become my primary "special interest".

I'll never forget my first radio show. My show directly followed an individual who eventually went on to become a professional broadcaster. He had the voice most broadcasters would give their front teeth for; very deep, velvety, and what's more, he thoroughly knew what he was talking about. For all intents and purposes he was good enough to be a DJ on national public radio (which he eventually became).

© 2005 Nicolas W. Dubin

A Jewish boy with a nasal voice, who knew next to nothing about jazz, was to follow this golden voice! Why couldn't someone else follow him?

"I feel really nervous," I told him in the studio. "I don't feel like I know a lot about the music I'm going to be playing."

"That's okay," he said. "Just pretend like you do. Go on feeling like you know everything about jazz."

The microphone was turned over to me and I read my script word for word. I must have sounded more like a music-history professor than a radio DJ. Every word I delivered on the air came from a script I had written out.

For the first six months I would script out entire shows. As I began to build my jazz collection and play the music every week, I became increasingly knowledgeable about jazz. Eventually I felt comfortable talking without a script. I knew so much about jazz that if I heard someone play, within three notes I'd know exactly who it was.

This was a much better experience for me than my announcing days in high school. There I was expected to conform to class standards by playing "their" music. In college I could play "I'll be Glad When You're Dead, You Rascal You" and people thought it was cool. In high school I had to use the difficult "reel-to-reel," whereas in college, I didn't. Had that been a requirement I don't think I could have had my own show. The fine motor manipulation would have been too challenging for me.

My radio show was the primary extracurricular activity I engaged in during school. Most of my classes were in the area of communication and involved interpersonal and group dialoguing, which I did not enjoy.

Breaking Through Hidden Barriers

I often wondered why I didn't just go to a school of broadcasting to learn the trade. Then I could bypass these classes where I had to interact so intensely with others. But I had already started down the path of obtaining a degree and it seemed futile to drop out at this point. So I stuck it out.

During those years I did not date. I did not socialize. I went to school, had my radio show, and worked as a tennis instructor. Those were my three basic life activities.

Although I had been teaching tennis since my junior year of high school, I still found it extremely difficult. It never seemed to get any easier for me. The emotional drain never seemed to positively outweigh the paycheck.

What drained me? Mostly, social interaction! The number one requirement (besides being able to teach the game of tennis) is to be a competent banterer. The tennis court is one of the most social environments known to man, other than perhaps the golf course. Look around the tennis courts or at a country club and what do you see? People having a good time, enjoying life, and being social!

My point is, you cannot be ill at ease socially and expect teaching tennis to be a breeze. Interacting with both tennis professionals and club members was excruciatingly challenging. A member would make a sarcastic joke and I wouldn't know how to respond. The staff would joke around with one another and I always seemed to be left out of the loop. Even in my "supposed milieu" on the tennis court my social difficulties would create problems. Consequently, teaching tennis was not enjoyable for me. It wasn't because I didn't love the game

© 2005 Nicolas W. Dubin

of tennis or that I was an incompetent pro. It was the socializing!

I could never justifiably explain to my parents why teaching tennis wasn't enjoyable for me. I used to say things like, "it drains me emotionally," or "I don't think it brings out the best in me." Then I'd hear things like, "Well, what else would you do at this phase in your life, work at a fast food restaurant?" They had a point there, I'll give them that. The idea of flipping burgers in a hot steamy environment, and having to do twenty million things at once (take orders, give change, remember orders, alternate between the drive-through and the counter), made teaching tennis seem like a walk in the park. My parents told me to count my blessings. I had a specialty skill which kept me out of that environment, even if I didn't love my job. As much as I didn't want to admit they were right, I had no choice. My parents *usually* (and I stress the word usually) make very good sense!

In the summer of 2000, I realized I was going to prepare to graduate and had not fully cemented my career goals. This bothered me greatly, and made me lose sleep on more than one occasion.

I had decided by this point that going into the field of radio was unrealistic. My reasoning was threefold:
1. It probably required too much extroversion.
2. The job itself is low-paying, unless you are in the top 1% of those in the business.
3. It is a very competitive business. A rookie DJ starts out in rural areas before moving to the big city, and even then there are no guarantees. Turnover rates in radio are extremely high.

Having eliminated radio as a career possibility, I had left myself in a precarious position. Banking on radio for four years, I had suddenly left myself without any career alternatives. I was in a panic.

I had considered many possibilities, from being a lawyer, to starting my own business, to being a teacher. Dad and I took a trip to Atlanta when I thought I wanted to be a school counselor. I had a fixation with the city of Atlanta. I didn't have any relatives who lived there but I liked the suburbs. I was going to move to a new city and start a program on the sole fact I liked the physical layout of the suburbs. Talk about not having my priorities in tact. In retrospect, I clearly see now that this was Aspie-like behavior.

After I came to my senses and eliminated Atlanta, I reasoned I would try to find a master's degree program around Detroit. I knew I wasn't socially or emotionally ready for any workplace, and the university setting would need to continue to act as my sanctuary.

One day I drove around the city of Detroit looking for a college program that might be compatible with my bachelor's degree. I looked into ten different programs at three colleges. One of the programs I stumbled upon was a master's degree in special education at the University of Detroit-Mercy. Since I had a documented learning disability, I thought I could possibly offer a lot as a special education teacher.

Dad and I made an appointment with the advisor of the program. She looked at my transcript and said I most likely would be admitted. The program was three years long, because I would have to take required undergraduate education classes. Normally a master's degree takes two years to complete, but the extra year seemed worth it if the career worked out.

© 2005 Nicolas W. Dubin

Within less than a week, I decided to apply for this program. Shortly after applying, I received a letter of acceptance and was about to begin a new and unexpected journey.

Chapter 7

Graduate School

I can only describe my graduate years as a time of self-discovery. I relished the fact I did not have to enter a workplace setting full-time. It meant I could spend more time reading books, spending time alone and discovering who I was. Most of these years were spent in solitude, with the exception of when I tried to step into the dating arena. During these years, I would come closer to discovering my diagnosis of Asperger's Syndrome.

I entered this program like a fish out of water. Most of the other students were full-time teachers who had been in the schools for a few years. The average age of the other students was early to middle thirties with some students being in their fifties. Class discussions would often focus on what teachers faced in their classrooms, leaving me little room for contribution. This was not my first experience feeling like I was in the minority.

In spite of this, I began to flourish academically. The kid who could barely get by in middle school was now regularly receiving A's and an occasional B. I would end up graduating Magna Cum Laude with a grade point above 3.7.

My theory of socialization during these years was that eventually it would get easier as I desensitized myself. I thought if I put myself in enough social situations I would naturally learn social skills. This was what my parents thought, and it seemed like common sense.

© 2005 Nicolas W. Dubin

Unfortunately, socializing didn't get easier even when I put myself in intense social situations. In the summer of 2002, I took a trip to England as part of a "study abroad" program connected to my master's program. I did this because it was a way for me to take three classes in three weeks that I would otherwise not be able to take.

This kind of trip is an Aspie's nightmare. It lasted three long weeks. There was an itinerary over which I had no control, I had to live within close quarters with people, I had virtually no privacy, and it was a noisy environment. These three weeks were a great test for me.

It all started when Mom and Dad dropped me off at the Windsor (Ontario) airport to bid me farewell. As we were driving to the airport I remember my stomach sinking. I would again be losing my freedom; with no car and no solitude, I would be at the mercy of everyone else. Why was this trip to England making me feel more depressed? Shouldn't something like this be a dream rather than a burden? Even I couldn't understand it. I should have been happy to go, but I wasn't. Was something wrong with me? I wondered.

The small talk started at the airport; yap, yap, yap. I could barely keep up with the conversations. They were talking so fast. I remember feeling that this would be three intense weeks of the most agonizing social pressures I'd ever faced in my life. I wasn't sure if I was up to the challenge.

On the flight to Toronto I was lucky enough to get a seat by myself. "Okay," I thought. "At least I'll have an hour and a half to regroup before it all starts again." But we had to deplane when we landed in Toronto, which meant socializing in the terminal as we waited for our next flight.

Everyone's spirits were jumping. Yap, yap, yap, yap! All I could think about was trying to get an empty seat on the plane to London. I went to the back of the plane and found a seat that was unoccupied. I suppose I shouldn't have done that because my assigned seat was with the group. I just remember feeling the peace and quiet of being alone on that plane with my book. That was enough for me. I was relieved I wouldn't have to sit next to someone for the next seven hours. Of course, when we landed in London everyone had to ask the obligatory question, "Where were you on the plane?"

Now the true test would begin. A bunch of taxis came and took us to our college in Oxford where we would stay for the next three weeks. Dad had arranged it so I could have a private room with a bathroom, something that was an absolute must. Everyone else had at least two other roommates with a communal bathroom. That would have been an intolerable situation for me.

Looking back, there was one moment during the trip that epitomized for me what it's like to have Asperger's Syndrome. The whole class, including our professors, decided to go to a pub one night after class. Everyone was having a jolly good time drinking, listening to loud music, and socializing. It was the Fourth of July so our group was especially festive.

At midnight the professors bought each person in our group a "shot" of alcohol to drink. Everyone was going to hold up a shot and gulp it down at the same time. I do not drink alcohol, and the thought of gulping down a shot was utterly terrifying. Now that I know I have Asperger's Syndrome, when I reflect on this situation as I

© 2005 Nicolas W. Dubin

realize I was afraid the shot would take away my sense of control. It is well discussed in literature that people with Asperger's need to feel in control of circumstances that might be unpredictable in nature. A shot would certainly make things unpredictable and I wasn't having any of that.

"C'mon Dubin", they all said. "Just drink it."

"I really don't want to", I whispered timidly.

Even my professor was encouraging me to drink, but I couldn't do it. I watched everyone drink a shot while I stood back as an observer.

During the time I wasn't in class or on-site at a school, I would spend time by myself. These moments in solitude weren't so horrific. I would walk up and down the streets of Oxford enjoying the sights alone. I'd see the daily beggar in the street singing and playing his guitar for nickels and dimes. I'd see the preacher trying to save souls. I'd watch and observe cultural differences between English and American people. This was all quite fascinating.

A lot of my time was spent taking walks along the Thames River. These walks cleansed my soul. I'd walk along the three-mile trail enjoying beautiful forestry. I'd peek in at the local game of croquet being played in the fields. I'd watch the elder citizens fish with their grandchildren. I would sometimes sit on the benches along the trail and simply take in the scenery. It was beautiful. I could have walked along that river all day.

When I wasn't walking along the river or spending time alone I was forced to be in social situations. Socializing was truly tiring for me. During this trip I consciously recognized for the first time I had a difference in this area. But I couldn't quite put a finger on it. Maybe I was an extreme introvert, or a schizoid. I just didn't know. All I knew was that this trip highlighted the significant differences I have when it comes to socializing.

Another way I tried desensitizing myself socially during these years was to enter the dating arena. Everyone in my family-- including myself-- was starting to wonder why I hadn't started dating. I was beginning to worry that if I didn't do this soon, I might never have a family. Common knowledge is that it gets more difficult to find a mate after leaving the confines of college.

I decided to use the computer as a vehicle to find a date rather than meeting someone on campus. My unconscious rationale was that perhaps I could enter the date with a fresh slate rather than with a person who had already witnessed my social foibles.

The first website I went to was a Jewish dating website. After three or four hours of searching I came across the profile of a young lady who seemed to fit the bill. First, she was Jewish. Second, she was black, and I liked African Americans. As if that wasn't enough, she was a jazz singer. She was a singer in a big band that performed standards from the Great American Songbook! I thought maybe this was fate; it seemed cosmically destined.

I wrote Karen an introductory email and within minutes she sent me an instant message. Jazz was the perfect introductory segue for our online conversation

"I noticed that in your profile, you said you're a jazz singer?" I asked.

"Yeah", Karen said.

"Jazz is like an addiction for me. I can't get enough of it."

"Really?" she asked. "Who do you like?" I

© 2005 Nicolas W. Dubin

proceeded to give her a laundry list of some of the people in jazz who I listened to.

"Wow", she said. "You do know a lot about jazz! I'm impressed."

We had several online conversations following this initial one. While emailing Karen, I was beginning to notice that communicating online was much easier than by telephone or face-to-face. Many intangibles present in face-to-face communication (such as the nonverbal element) are not present in typewritten communications. Responses can be deliberate and calculated since there's more time to think about what to say, as opposed to verbally responding immediately. For Aspies it is well documented that sensory processes can be impaired. I think this is why many Aspies take longer in formulating their responses. They need more time to decode the information that has been communicated and more time to formulate a response. As a result, they may appear to come across as "academic" or pedantic.

Sooner or later, I knew that my correspondence with Karen would have to evolve beyond instant messages. I wanted to keep online correspondence going as long as possible to mold a favorable impression in her mind. Apparently Karen enjoyed our conversations, and after about a month of talking online, she asked if I would call her. This made me very nervous but I knew I had no choice if I ever was to "date" this woman.

I called her and made the conversation as quick as possible. Again, my approach was conservative because I didn't want any of my social foibles to be exposed before the date. The plan was to meet at a restaurant about an hour away from where I lived.

I remember thinking even before our first date that I might eventually marry Karen. Most people would consider that a little premature, but I didn't think so at the time. In my mind this was the opportunity of a lifetime and I had to take advantage of it. I went to a florist on my way and bought her a bouquet of roses. I realize now that was rushing it a bit, but as far as I was concerned, buying bouquets of roses was the sort of thing people did on first dates.

To make a long story short, the date was a flop. Karen looked like a bolt of lightening hit her when I gave her the roses. It was not the look of "love at first sight" which I had expected, but was more along the lines of, "This feels freaky." After the date I emailed her and asked her if she wanted to go on another date. I never heard back from her. To say that I was crushed would be an understatement.

Another date during that three year period was with a girl named Jessie. A friend of my Mom's fixed us up. The plan was to pick her up and we would head to a jazz club. Conversation was sparse throughout the date and I was the one who initiated most of the dialogue between us. By the time I dropped her off that night, I was completely exhausted.

I emailed Jessie the next day asking her if she wanted to go out again the following weekend. Three or four days passed without hearing back from her. I began thinking maybe she didn't want to go out again, which in turn gave way to feelings of rage. This would be the fourth time someone had rejected me without responding. So I wrote Jessie another email lecturing her about how inconsiderate she was for not responding to my first email. I said something to the effect of,

© 2005 Nicolas W. Dubin

"You know, if you don't want to go out with me, the decent thing would be to say so. It's completely rude for you to ignore me."

I got an email back saying,

"Who do you think you are? No, I do not want to go out with you again! So there, are you happy?"

Once again, I was crushed. I felt like I had blown it for the umpteenth time.

Finally, I met a girl named Melissa who seemed to show interest in me. I met her through another internet Jewish dating website. Our dates together exhausted me to the point that when they were over, I had to immediately go to sleep.

Melissa was the talker and I was the listener throughout our brief three month relationship. To my credit I felt that I tried to be there for her. I always made a concerted effort to seem interested in what she had to say and who she was as a person. In retrospect, she was not my type. Melissa was into pop-culture, gossip, current fashion trends, and the like. I think the reason I liked her was because she was appearing to show interest in me.

After three months her apparent interest dissipated into thin air and the relationship fell apart. Much of this was due to my lack of experience in the dating arena and my as yet undiscovered Asperger's. For example, Melissa and I went to several movies on our dates. At one of the movies Melissa leaned over and put her hand on top of mine. Immediately my whole body tensed up. I didn't know how to respond to her gesture of affection and my first instinct was to tighten up my muscles. I never reciprocated by putting my hand on top of hers. At the time I didn't even think of doing so. What brought this to my attention was when I told Dad that she had put her hand on mine.

"Well I assume you put your arm around her or held her hand in return?" he asked.

Truth was, it didn't even enter my mind. Talk about missing social cues.

Things began spiraling out of control a few months into the relationship. Melissa had invited me to her best friend's wedding and the party afterwards was at a fancy banquet hall. What did this mean for me? An extremely uncomfortable situation! I know going to a wedding knowing only your date would be uncomfortable for most people, but it was particularly uncomfortable for me.

I was totally over-stimulated by the noise of the party. The tapestry of socializing was too intense for me. After the first five minutes I was ready for a nap. I remember Melissa ignoring me, which made me a little upset. She knew I was a rather shy person and she wasn't making any attempt to help me feel comfortable. By 10:00 p.m., I had to leave. Melissa made the obligatory walk with me to my car, kissed me on the cheek, and went back to the banquet hall.

The next day we were supposed to go out together. I was going to pick her up around 1:00 p.m.. Instead, at 12:30 I received a message on my answering machine.

"Hi Nick; it's Melissa. Instead of you coming here today, I'm going to come to your place at 1:00. See you then."

Intuitively, I knew the reason she was coming over was to break up with me. I could feel it in the air, particularly by the way I was treated the night before at

© 2005 Nicolas W. Dubin

the wedding. I asked her why she no longer wanted to see me and she responded that I was basically a stiff pickle. I wasn't any fun to be with, and I didn't bring out her wild and crazy side. Again, she kissed me on the check and then she was gone, out of my life forever.

I had mixed feelings about the breakup. On one hand, I was crushed and devastated because this was one more person I could add to my rejection list. On the other hand, I was relieved. I felt like a burden had been lifted off my shoulders. My days weren't so draining and I had more energy. "Could it be I'm just not destined to live the married life?" I asked myself.

Okay, so I would never be a social butterfly or the life of the party, but I still have to function in the real world and this requires socializing. I remember asking my parents on a trip to Cleveland not too long ago, shortly before discovering my Asperger's:

"Mom and Dad, do you guys think I'll ever be able to maintain permanent employment as an adult?"

"Honey, why would you ask that? You're a bright, capable person," Mom said.

"I know but something just seems to be awry with me. I can't put my finger on it."

"You have nothing to worry about, Nick", Dad said in his characteristically reassuring tone. "There are a lot of people in the world who are not nearly as bright as you, and they are out there making good and decent livings. Honestly, this is the last thing you should worry about."

The logic was unfaltering. After all, I was getting a 3.7 in graduate school, writing sophisticated research papers with relative ease, and handling graduate school without much trouble. Removing the hidden barriers of

Asperger's from the equation, there would be no reason in the world I should struggle in the "real world".

Glimpses of the "struggle" I'm alluding to started coming to fruition during my graduate years. Besides struggling socially, I made a number of embarrassing mistakes. One time when I was teaching tennis I ran a tournament. I put two incorrect matches on the court not at all aware that the people I sent off to play were the wrong opponents for each other. A spectator approached me and pointed this out forty-five minutes into the matches. I had to recall the matches and reassign different opponents to the four players. It was an embarrassing scene, and needless to say, the parents were upset with me.

Another time I had to open up the club for a big tournament early in the morning. I had the only key and I could not get the lock open for some reason. With fifty people standing around me, I had to ask a parent to open the lock. I could hear a few giggles in the background, reminiscent of that infamous incident in second grade when I was unable to open the door.

Another time a twelve year old girl who appeared to have paint on her face was taking tennis lessons on my court. I was curious and went ahead and asked her,

"Did you decide to paint your face for some reason?"

"Uh, no......." she said.

"Oh, well what happened to your face?" I asked innocently.

She stared at me for a few moments and then ran away crying. I couldn't figure it out until later when one of the pros told me the girl had some sort of a skin disease.

© 2005 Nicolas W. Dubin

I'm sure I appeared grossly insensitive to her, although it certainly was not my intent.

Those mistakes and others of a similar nature started to concern me as to my functionality in the world. In other words, could I function properly as a person of humanity? This concern would be increasingly magnified toward the end of my graduate years during my student teaching experience.

The culmination of my master's degree studies at the University of Detroit involved student teaching. I was required to student teach for two semesters; one in a general education classroom and the other in a special education classroom.

I was doing very well academically as I embarked on my student teaching experience. My grade point average of 3.7 should have foreshadowed a successful student teaching experience. That did not turn out to be the case.

I was placed in a second grade classroom. My cooperating teacher, Julie, was around my age. She had been selected student teacher of the year in Michigan three years earlier, and she was a real perfectionist. The first time I met her I could tell this was the case because the room was super organized! In the beginning there was no reason for her to believe I would cause any problems as a student teacher. My interview went well with both her and the principal of the school, and Julie enthusiastically welcomed me into her classroom.

Even though I was nervous to begin my student teaching I couldn't have possibly imagined how badly it would go for me. My worst case scenario was a fairy tale compared to what actually happened. It was here that my Aspieness shone through like it never had before.

Although I did not know it at the time, Asperger's Syndrome affected me during student teaching in the following ways:
1. Huge difficulty multitasking
2. Difficulty manipulating classroom materials due to fine motor difficulties. (Fine motor difficulties can be a characteristic of Asperger's Syndrome)
3. Difficulty with sociability, especially with other faculty.
4. Extreme difficulty being aware of the needs of every child in the class.

It's been said that a classroom teacher makes hundreds, if not thousands, of small decisions per day in his or her classroom. This translates to several decisions every few minutes. The ability to multitask is essential for a teacher.

Multitasking is the ability to be aware of one's peripheral environment and do several things simultaneously. This means one's attention must be focused in a number of different directions at the same time. This is a difficult skill for anyone, but for many people with Asperger's Syndrome, it can be nearly impossible —and it was for me. As a student teacher I had to be aware of several things at once. Here's an example of what a teacher might have to do simultaneously:
A. Take attendance.
B. Make sure Johnny keeps his hands off Cindy.
C. Answer someone who keeps yelling out "Mr. Dubin, Mr. Dubin!!"
D. Write something on the board.
E. Get the overhead projector ready for the next lesson.

I think you get the idea.

© 2005 Nicolas W. Dubin

I quickly found out as a student teacher that multitasking was a near impossibility for me. I was simply overwhelmed by the quantity of demands in my immediate environment. I felt like saying "Go away, I can't take this anymore!" Because of my difficulty multitasking, I was constantly making mistakes.

People with Asperger's Syndrome are often unidirectional creatures. That means they love to be immersed with one thing at a time so they can put their heart and soul into it. They may not be aware of everything going on in their environment, but they are completely aware of what's within their tunnel vision. Outside of their tunnel vision, within the peripheral environment, they may be completely impervious. That definitely applies to me. I'm a unidirectional creature. Consequently, I found the multitasking element of the classroom completely overwhelming.

The second difficulty I had in the classroom was manipulating the classroom materials. As a second grade teacher one must be at least minimally proficient in performing basic tasks with one's hands. Fine motor skills are a necessity for teaching primary grades.

My fine motor skills were embarrassingly bad. After school one day Julie asked me to tie string onto a hook that would stretch down from the ceiling for each student. Attached to the hooks was supposed to be artwork the students designed for parents to see at the "open house". I struggled with the string and hook for a few minutes until Julie finally asked me what the problem was. I told her I was having trouble tying the string around the hook but I would keep trying, and she gave me a very bizarre look. Minutes later she relieved me of that duty and had me do clerical work on the computer--

something I was more comfortable with. I was embarrassed that I could not do something as simple as tie a string around a hook.

Other tasks that involved fine motor skills were problematic as well. Stapling a piece of paper onto a bulletin board was something I couldn't figure out until I was shown. Even then I still struggled with it. I felt completely inept.

I was at a complete loss in the copy room. I inadvertently misused the copy machine a number of times by putting paper in the wrong place or pressing the wrong button even after being shown the correct way to use the machine.

Writing on the board was another challenge due to poor fine motor skills. The comments I made on a student's work would often be illegible due to my sloppy handwriting. I tried compensating for my handwriting by making transparencies in advance. Many times I'd lose them or put them in the wrong order. Again, because I felt like I had to be on top of a million things at the same time something as simple as keeping transparencies in order became a challenge for me.

Sociability was another problem for me. At lunch I needed a break, so I would leave the school building. I would later find out this was frowned upon by the teachers. If I didn't have time for myself during that forty-five minute period I probably would have collapsed or fainted. I needed time to myself at lunch like we all need oxygen to breathe.

I could tell being a teacher was a job that required interpersonal connectivity and sociability. This was an area that I was (and still am) lacking in a great degree. I found myself uncomfortable in the teachers lounge and on the playground where other teachers gathered to socialize. I remember thinking this would be a huge challenge for me as a teacher.

Lastly, I seemed to have a hard time of simultaneously being aware of every student's needs. Simply put, I was having trouble sorting out what individual students needed in terms of remediation.

Behaviorally speaking, I was also unaware of student needs. I might not notice Johnny punching Jim in the back of the classroom because I was so preoccupied with what I was doing at the time. Most likely this directly correlated with my difficulty in multitasking.

Julie was constantly criticizing me, and she rarely had anything positive to say. I was frustrating her and she made no secret about that. She had talked to the principal and called my supervising professor at the university a couple of times. I was feeling like a failure in every conceivable way and was scared that maybe I had chosen the wrong profession.

I remember one day after school let out, everyone had left the building and I stayed in the classroom and bawled my eyes out. I cried myself a river in that classroom. I was feeling like I had to let go of a dream I had been holding onto for the past three years. I poured my heart and soul into this program and I was throwing it away. Something in my soul told me I was in the wrong place physically, spiritually, emotionally, and mentally.

I knew that I had a difficult choice to make. I could continue student teaching (and probably fail the course) or I could quit. If I quit, what would I do with my life? Would my master's degree be for naught? Would I even receive my master's degree? Would the 3.7 grade point I worked so hard to achieve be thrown out the window?

Staring at myself in the mirror, I knew if I continued with the student teaching, I might have literally committed suicide. My wiser self was gently trying to tell me this wasn't the right profession for me and I had to find some way to let go. I resisted until I couldn't any longer. I simply had no choice. It was too intolerable for me, so I officially threw in the towel.

I received full support from the principal of the school and in fact, he assured me I was making the right choice. Julie felt like she failed me. I know she cared about me and wanted my experience to go well and I was obviously grateful to her. In the end I made a clean break and went back the drawing board.

Now I was faced with a tough predicament. I had thrown away the possibility of receiving a teaching certificate, which was the intended goal when I entered the program. The only hope I had was that maybe I could still obtain the master's degree. After all, I had completed my coursework. The only prerequisite I had not fulfilled was the student teaching, which exists primarily so one can become licensed to teach. At this point, I knew getting licensed just wasn't going to happen.

I decided to go to the dean and explain my situation. For good measure, I asked my dad to accompany me. He was (and is) a law professor at the University of Detroit Mercy and I felt his presence would help put some pressure on them. I wasn't trying to manipulate the situation but in truth, I was desperate. I was willing to do anything. Without the master's degree, I would have wasted three years of schooling and I wasn't quite ready to do that.

© 2005 Nicolas W. Dubin

Dad and I met with Sister Anne and I explained my situation. I told her I had done well academically but my student teaching experience was a disaster. I said that I really gave it my all and it just didn't work out, for whatever reason. I asked her if I could still receive my master's degree since I had completed all the other required coursework. My jaw clenched and my muscles tightened as I waited for her response. The future of my existence depended on what Sister Anne was going to say.

To my astonishment, Sister Anne told me I had completed everything to receive the master's degree. She said not everyone pursues a teaching certificate. Some people just go for the academic degree. She was very compassionate and understanding of what I had just gone through.

Amazingly, I graduated the University of Detroit Mercy Magna Cum Laude with a master's degree in special education. Now the only question was what to do next!

My life had been thrown into a major tailspin with the disappointment of not completing student teaching. On an existential level I felt like this event had destroyed all meaning in my life. For three weeks after I quit student teaching I did not leave my apartment. I sank into a deep depression. I felt like committing suicide. I felt lost, like a sailor on dry land. I just didn't know what I was going to do with my life.

One thing I did know was I couldn't do much with a master's degree in special education without the vital teaching certificate. I learned that most jobs outside of teaching in the schools required many years of teaching experience, which I would never accumulate. It basically meant I had a glorified degree. Sure, it was a master's degree, but if I couldn't get work, what good would it do me?

I now had to begin the process of searching for a career all over again, just like I did after getting my bachelor's degree. This time, I knew I was going to be a little more deliberate in terms of searching than I was the first time. I wouldn't pick a school based on a city's nice suburbs. I wouldn't haphazardly choose a career to fill a void or out of sheer panic. No, this time I would do it wisely. I would not make the same mistake twice!

I began thinking about things I could do. What were my talents and skills? I looked into programs that might accept my master's degree. Unfortunately, all the programs I searched required taking the Graduate Record Exam (GRE), which was something I dreaded. On top of that, in order to qualify to get into many programs, I basically would have to get another bachelor's degree in another field.

Then one day I came upon a program on the internet that looked intriguing. The program was in humanistic and clinical psychology and offered what's called a Psy.D, which is a doctorate in psychology. I scrupulously looked at the requirements for admittance into the program and to my sheer delight they did not require the GRE or an outside degree. Since education is a related field to psychology it would mean I was eligible to apply for a doctorate degree. I was ecstatic because psychology had become one of my "special interests." I made a comment to Dad during my student teaching that I wished I had chosen psychology as a career. Now here was my chance! I had to see if I could get in! I remember filling out my application as if I was sending a note to

Santa Claus. My adrenaline was pumping as I considered the possibilities associated with getting a doctoral degree. It was as if I was going through momentary amnesia of my student teaching experience.

I discovered there was a highly interpersonal aspect to the program. It was not the kind of program where one goes to class, takes notes, and leaves. Instead, students get to know each other on a very deep level. I considered this a "red flag" and debated whether or not I should attend the initial interview. I eventually decided to just go for it.

I would be accepted into the program if I took three prerequisite classes in psychology and completed a clinical training. I felt very hesitant to sign on the dotted line but it was an opportunity I couldn't let slip by.

I had finally found a path. The trouble was, I wasn't entirely comfortable with it.

Chapter 8

Discovering Asperger's Syndrome

After I was accepted into the program at the Center for Humanistic Studies, I went on a reading rampage. I began reading everything I could about psychology, hoping to gain valuable insights into myself. I remember specifically what triggered the "reading rampage".

I decided to teach tennis again because I needed some income. Someone I had been playing tennis with for several years hired me as his assistant at a country club. We had known each other for seven or eight years and were pretty good friends through tennis.

One day when I was at the club I noticed a real uneasiness about being with people. I knew that it wasn't just social anxiety. It seemed to go beyond that. I was definitely feeling a distinct social barrier between myself and others, yet it was unseen and certainly not tangible. It was the lack of fluidity in my relating to people. People wouldn't joke around with me like they would with others. The conversations were stiff and people tended to not "open up" to me. When I say "open up", I don't mean on any deep psychological level. I'm talking about trivial things. I suddenly became aware it wasn't just happening at this particular country club, it had been going on my whole life.

It was becoming obvious to me that something was definitely different about me. I couldn't understand it though, because I had never come across anything in my psychological reading about being "socially different." I had only read about introverts, shyness, social anxiety, and the like. Now was my time to investigate and get to the bottom of this. I wanted something to explain everything in my life; why I was the way I was. I wanted to "know myself" better, because I felt like a complete enigma.

So I started buying a slew of books; self-help books, psychology books, anything that might give me insight into myself. Shyness didn't explain it to my satisfaction, nor did introversion, social anxiety, or learning disabilities. I began feeling depressed that there were no rational explanations as to why I was the way I was.

On one trip to the bookstore I came across a book about Asperger's Syndrome. I was reading about Asperger's in a prerequisite class at the time and I had remembered hearing about it in one of my special education courses. But I always associated it with autism. The first time I passed the book in the store I paid it little attention. Just the fact that the word "autism" was connected with Asperger's made me conclude rather quickly that it didn't apply to me. But time after time I would pass the book and it would always catch my eye. Finally, my curiosity got the best of me and I had to take a look at it. My initial thought was, "Yeah right, autistic? This will be a quick look."

After about fifteen minutes of reading about Asperger's Syndrome, my jaw dropped to the floor. I said very audibly in the store, "Hallelujah!" Similar to the way Yogis or Monks attain enlightenment in a seemingly timeless moment of bliss, I felt like this was my moment of enlightenment. It was a very emotional moment for me and I almost burst into tears of joy. I felt validated and vindicated in some ways.

Breaking Through Hidden Barriers

As I continued to read, I noticed the features of Asperger's Syndrome that applied to me. They were:
1. Speech delay as a child
2. Poor fine motor skills
3. Loner
4. Significant difference between verbal and performance scores on IQ tests
5. Difficulty multitasking
6. Unidirectional
7. Sensitivity to sound
8. Easily over stimulated
9. Having very focalized special interests! (history of tennis, jazz, game shows, expressways, psychology, studying things of a psychical nature, etc)
10. Struggling socially all my life!

I knew I had found my answer in Asperger's Syndrome. It was almost too good to be true and certainly unbelievable! I had to share the good news with Mom and Dad.

Initially they didn't take the news like I would have hoped. They also knew that Asperger's was associated with autism, and didn't believe that applied to me. After discussing my new discovery with them, I learned that my mother had called a neuropsychologist to help her understand my struggles during student teaching. My mother was beginning to wonder the same thing I was. We were all trying to make the same discovery after my disastrous student teaching, whether we were consciously aware of it or not.

After awhile my parents started to take my claims seriously. My mother called the same neuropsychologist once again and explained to him I suspected I had Asperger's Syndrome. He agreed to see me.

When I first met Dr. Milanovich, he interviewed both my parents and me. From his initial intake he said it sounded like I could be a candidate for the syndrome but there was no real substantive way to prove it unless he gave me a battery of tests. We gave him results from tests I had taken over the years, which would hopefully help with the current results. I agreed to take the tests.

The testing lasted ten hours. It was grueling and painfully exhausting. When I left Dr. Milanovich's office after the third day of testing, he said we would meet with my parents in a few days to discuss the results.

One of the other reasons I wanted to see this neuropsychologist was to know if going into a career in psychology was wise if indeed, I had Asperger's. After all, being aware of someone's needs is pretty paramount in terms of being a good psychotherapist.

During the testing, Dr. Milanovich and I began talking on a personal level. He asked me directly if I wanted to be a psychotherapist. I told him I didn't feel totally comfortable with the idea particularly after what happened with my student teaching experience. I felt pretty certain I had Asperger's Syndrome and if this was the case, it probably wouldn't be in anyone's best interests. But this created another crisis; if I did have Asperger's Syndrome would I have to bow out of my psychology program where I had already been accepted to pursue a doctorate? The idea was nauseating. Still, I did not want to enter a program if I wasn't going to be well suited for it.

Mom, Dad and I drove up to Ann Arbor on a Tuesday to meet with Dr. Milanovich for an hour and a half. We were going to get answers and hopefully become enlightened as to the mystery of Nick Dubin. But it was no longer truly a mystery. We were all quite certain that provide a positive diagnosis of Asperger's. And that's exactly what happened.

Dr. Milanovich explained that my profile was absolutely consistent with what's called a "Nonverbal learning disability". I scored very low on tests that required me to make sense of pictures by putting them in sequential order. I also did poorly on tests that required fine motor manipulation and on tests involving visual short term and long term memory. However, I scored extremely well on tests of verbal ability. This discrepancy was consistent with the differential gap I had scored on tests taken years ago. We learned that this gap was the cognitive profile of a nonverbal learning disability. This was news to both my folks and me.

He explained that when he looked at both the nonverbal learning disability and my social history it clearly showed a diagnosis of Asperger's. He was very reassuring to me that there was no doubt in his mind, as he could see I was probing him to give me that certainty.

The next question was obvious; should I pursue this doctoral degree in psychology? He retorted by asking a question right back:

"Nick, what do you want to do right now career wise?"

Now, here's the funny part about all this. I had been asking myself that question everyday for the past eight years and never had a real answer. But the moment he asked me that question, I knew what the answer was. It was suddenly obvious to me. I answered:

"I think I want to be an advocate for those with

Asperger's. I have a degree in special education."

"But you don't want to do therapy, right?" he asked.

"Absolutely not!", I said emphatically.

"I agree with you", he said. "I think it would be incredibly taxing and draining for you." "But, I do see some incredible possibilities for you. I think you could make a real difference in the lives of people if you choose this path."

"But do you think I should pursue this degree?"

"That's something you have to talk about with the school. You'll have to disclose this information and give them the report I'm going to write up for you."

"What are you going to say in the report?" I asked. "Well, I'm going to say that in terms of internships, I think intense interpersonal contact through therapy with others would be difficult if near impossible for you. However, I do see you working as a co-facilitator for social skills groups of people with Asperger's. I could also see you giving speeches at various schools to parents and teachers. I would even offer you an internship to work with me!"

I was incredibly honored he offered that to me on the spot.

The student teaching situation came up during the conversation.

"You were obviously very impaired in the classroom", he said. "There's no question about that. In retrospect, I'm sure you wouldn't have chosen to work in an elementary classroom with the knowledge you have now."

"No sir, I certainly wouldn't have," I said.

For the first time in my life I felt completely whole. My sense of purpose and meaning suddenly became

Breaking Through Hidden Barriers

clear. My mission in life was clearly established. Suddenly, it made sense why I had to experience all of the hardships thus far in my life. I had to experience the pain of not opening the door in second grade; of not fitting in during my middle school years, of driving home through snow and sleet every weekend from college, of continually making embarrassing mistakes; of not completing student teaching. It all made sense now. I had found my path.

The process of "coming out" of my shell would now have to take place. I was going to have to disclose the neuropsych report to the school and alert them that I had Asperger's Syndrome. It was a lot to swallow considering I had just learned of my diagnosis only a month earlier.

This was what I planned to say to CHS:

"I want to work as a specialist in the area of Asperger's Syndrome as a professional psychologist. I was diagnosed with the Syndrome recently. My neuropsychologist has said he feels practicing therapy would not be in my best interest since it would not utilize my skills. However, he does see me as having a positive impact in the area of Asperger's".

These were the questions I planned to ask CHS:

A. Do you think it would be feasible to attend school here without the goal of being a therapist?
B. Could I have alternative internships/ practicum, rather than the traditional therapy practicum?

My parents and I went to meet with the administrative staff. At first, there seemed to be some hesitancy towards the idea but as the meeting continued they became more open. They said they would discuss it and get back to me in a few days.

A few days later I received an email stating they would be happy to have me enter their program. Not only were they looking forward to having me, but they said they could learn from me, in terms of information about Asperger's. I was overjoyed!

Chapter 9

Resolution and Some Final Thoughts

As I write this chapter I am beginning a brand new journey, embarking on a new chapter of my life. My life as a postgraduate student will hopefully be rewarding as I get to know more about myself, Asperger's Syndrome, and how I can be of service to others.

Having been diagnosed with Asperger's Syndrome for a short while now, I cannot honestly profess to be an expert. Hopefully, I'll get there someday. However there are a few things I have learned. One myth I've heard is:

"People with Asperger's Syndrome lack empathy".

Think about that for a moment. There are many prominent authors on the autism spectrum who share their knowledge and compassion to help individuals on the spectrum understand their importance in the world. It seems to me if these people were not empathic they wouldn't be out there trying to make a difference in the Asperger community. Instead, they would be wallowing in their own misery. It is empathy that calls them into service.

To me it isn't empathy we (Aspies) lack but it can be perceived that way. For example, recall the time when I asked the girl if she painted her face. It could have easily been perceived by her that I wasn't being empathetic. The rigidity of my thinking caused me to ask her, not my lack of empathy. If I wasn't aware of students' needs in the classroom, again, it was not lack of empathy, but rather tunnel vision, or that unidirectional mentality I referred to earlier. I think we need to dispel the myth that people with Asperger's do not feel or display empathy. We do, but in a different way. You just have to look below the surface.

People with Asperger's Syndrome have a different way of operating in the world compared to our neurotypical counterparts. We are like Frank Sinatra; we see things "our way". We operate within the context of seeing things through a particular lens. Our neurological wiring is such that we process things in a very personal way. We become intimately involved in whatever we are doing to the point where we sometimes lose sight of the big gestalt. In the classroom for example, I would become so focused on taking attendance or writing something on the board, I wasn't able to see what else was going on around me. Johnny could be punching Jimmy in the back of the room and I'd be oblivious to it. Many neurotypicals would have been able to take attendance while simultaneously answering a student's question, and tying another student's shoes. That wasn't possible for me but at least now I know why. I know that it has nothing to do with my overall intelligence or cognitive ability.

I'd really like people with Asperger's Syndrome to consider themselves as intelligent human beings. One of the things Big Bird from Sesame Street taught us as kids is that we are going to make mistakes. That's just par for the course. Everyone in life learns Big Bird's lesson. For people with Asperger's Syndrome that lesson gets intensified tenfold out in the world. It's very easy for us to reason that because we make so many "common sense" mistakes, we are unintelligent or defective in some way. I know, I thought that for a long time. Please...Please....I urge you not to! It's a fallacy. It would be as if someone

with glasses thought he/she was stupid because they had trouble reading an eye chart from a distance. We have trouble seeing the big picture in the same way others having trouble literally seeing through their own eyes. Forgive yourself! Don't waste another ounce of energy beating yourself over the head the next time you fail to see the whole gestalt in a particular situation. It's just the way you're wired. Instead, appreciate your strengths:
1. Maybe you have incredibly tenacity when it comes to things you're passionate about.
2. Maybe you can focus intensely on something for long periods of time, if it holds your interest.
3. Maybe you have unique perspectives or unusual ways of seeing the world, which can help to enhance those around you.
4. Maybe you have knowledge in a specialty area where you could really be of service to others.

I would urge anyone reading this book who suspects they might have Asperger's Syndrome to see a professional. I suggest you see a psychologist or a neuropsychologist who has familiarity with Asperger's Syndrome to discuss an evaluation. A psychologist is likely to rely on an interview and a history intake in making their diagnosis. He or she will generally go by the DSM criteria in diagnosing you.

When you see a neuropsychologist, not only is he or she going to do an intake, but you are also likely to take a series of tests that will measure your cognitive profile. The tests are laborious but please don't let that stop you from taking them. They are absolutely essential if you are serious about getting to the bottom of it all. If you seem to show the characteristics of a nonverbal learning disability (NLD) and you fit the DSM criteria for Asperger's, you will receive a pretty foolproof diagnosis.

The following would be my suggestions for preparations:
1. Get a good night sleep the night before the evaluation.
2. Take a family member with you who can give the professional an objective perspective of your social history.
3. Make sure you bring any previous test results from psychologists or educators with you. This will help the professional in making an accurate diagnosis.
4. Be as honest with the professional as possible. If you can't be honest, you will only be hurting yourself.
5. Do not see a professional until you are ready to handle the truth.

I would be remiss if I told you seeing a professional is not important if it truly is in your heart to do so. Getting a diagnosis can be a very cathartic experience. If the diagnosis is Asperger's you will have an explanation for much of what has taken place in your life. Those hidden barriers between you and others that seemed like a mystery over the years will finally be understood. If you do not receive a diagnosis of Asperger's, chances are you still exhibit Asperger-like tendencies, and having that information from a licensed professional would be helpful for you. Then you will know your perceived differences are not "all in your head."

Receiving a diagnosis is important only if it is important to you. If you feel it's irrelevant and knowing wouldn't help in any way, then don't do it. But if you feel

there's been a missing piece in your life that you want to possibly identify, then I urge you to obtain a formal diagnosis. The result will likely be:
1. You will forgive yourself on many levels.
2. You will finally be able to say "so this is what it was".
3. It will be easier for you to go forward in life with this piece of information.
4. You will know what occupations or jobs would be more suited to you.
5. It will be emotionally liberating on many different levels.

As I mentioned in number four one of the most important reasons to obtain a diagnosis is so you can find meaningful employment, and a viable career option. Without knowing that "it" is Asperger's you may continue with a career or start a new career that is clearly not suited to your strengths and talents. Clearly, if I had the Asperger diagnosis before I started student teaching, I probably wouldn't have student taught. That isn't to say someone with Asperger's Syndrome cannot be a teacher. What I'm saying is that as an individual, you need to pick a career where you can excel and take care of yourself at the same time. For example, if you know that socializing is taxing, don't sign up to be the social director of a cruise ship. A less extreme example is if you tire easily from socializing, you might not want to choose a job where you are with people nonstop from 9:00-5:00. You may need a job that provides some independence, where you can work on individual projects that inspire you. The kind of job and career you'll eventually select will depend entirely on the conclusions you come to after lengthy self-exploration, factoring Asperger's into the equation.

© 2005 Nicolas W. Dubin

If you have Asperger's Syndrome and are wondering what career or profession is for you, I'm sorry I don't have a definitive answer. It would be foolish for me to tell you to be a lawyer, scientist or engineer, because I do not know you personally. However, if you have Asperger's Syndrome I can assume some very general things about you and based upon the assumptions, these are my recommendations:

1. Choose a career that helps you utilize your "special interest". For example, if you have an intense interest in history, you might want to think about teaching at the high school or university level, or working in a museum. If your interest lies in the schedules of trains you might want to think about doing something with trains or statistics. If your interest is in rocks, think about being a geologist.
2. Choose a career that allows you to build upon your strengths. Pick a career or job where you are not going to be bombarded with many different things at the same time. Choose a job where you can intensely focus on one thing at a time; a job where multitasking is not a big component.
3. Choose a job where you feel comfortable enough to disclose your diagnosis to your employers, if you ever decide to do so.
4. Realize that no job is going to be perfect. But some jobs and careers are more "doable" than others for people with Asperger's.

One of the reasons many people are hesitant to pursue a diagnosis of Asperger's Syndrome is because it is connected with autism. There is a stigma connected with the word autism that often makes people feel uneasy when they hear Asperger's Syndrome connected to it. Both my parents and I first dismissed the notion that I could possibly have Asperger's because of its association with autism.

So I'd like to give my unsolicited opinion on the subject, which might help to put this in perspective for you. But first here are some facts:

Asperger's is generally considered to be part of the autism spectrum. Some professionals argue it is nothing more than a nonverbal learning disability; others say it's a form of pervasive developmental disorder, and still others say it is high functioning autism. There is a lot of disagreement in the autism/Asperger's community as to how one should actually categorize Asperger's. A lot of semantics come into play.

There is tremendous overlap between Asperger's and nonverbal learning disabilities, which has been well established in general literature. One can, however, have a nonverbal learning disability and not be diagnosed with Asperger's. There seems to be less overlap between NLD and autism than there is with Asperger's and autism. Here are a couple of reasons why Asperger's is considered to be part of the Autism Spectrum:

1. There are certain neurological soft signs that are found in autism which can also be found in Asperger's, that are generally not found in NLD. These soft signs include hand flapping, rocking back and forth, idiosyncratic behaviors, and other self-stimulating behaviors.
2. Those with NLD tend not to have the intensified special interests as those with Asperger's do. There is some overlap with this characteristic

© 2005 Nicolas W. Dubin

between Asperger's and autism. Some autistic individuals can tell you everything there is to know about a particular subject, having knowledge most experts probably wouldn't possess.
3. Now here comes my opinion of the subject. Yes, I do believe that Asperger's Syndrome falls on the high end of the autism spectrum. So do many well known individuals who speak publicly about Asperger's Syndrome. **But** (and this is a big but), as I mentioned in the preface of this book, we, as a society, need to reframe our ideas about autism. We need to stop thinking of everyone who has any form of autism as a "Rain Man" caricature and instead see people with Asperger's for who we really are. We are functional people who operate in a unique way and believe it or not, we could excel in the world under the right circumstances. We just need to be given that chance.

You know Asperger's Syndrome is considered a "shadow syndrome" for a reason. It is a "shadow" of autism. A shadow! Let me give you a few analogies that might put this into context for you:
1. An overeater is a shadow of a glutton.
2. Solitary people are shadows of schizoids.
3. Daydreamers, psychics and mystics could arguably be considered shadows of schizophrenics.
4. A religious person is a shadow of a fundamentalist.

So what's the point? The point is I hope you do not let the word "autism" stop you from pursuing an evaluation. If you think in the context of being a "shadow", you can understand intellectually that it is not at all like full blown autism. Unlike the Rainman character, you are not likely to insist on going to the K-Mart in Cincinnati the next time you need underwear. If you don't watch the People's Court or Jeopardy at a certain time each day your life isn't going to come to an end. I say these things in jest but the truth is that for a full blown autistic, these are not extreme examples, but may be a difficult reality.

Let's put it this way. On the continuum between autism and neurotypicals, we with Asperger's Syndrome are closer to the side of the neurotypicals. Yet, we have enough of the same characteristics (at a much milder level) as individuals diagnosed with autism and are considered a part of that spectrum. If anything, you can celebrate your accomplishments in life knowing you have a strain of autism inside your being! Give yourself a pat on the back! And please, try to reframe the word autism in your mind. I think that will help you mentally and psychologically before pursuing an evaluation.

If you have already been diagnosed with Asperger's and are reading this book, you know as well as I do that we are all unique individuals. What makes Asperger's such a tricky diagnosis is that there are so many contradictions. Some Aspies will talk your head off about their particular "special interests," while some will keep everything to themselves. Some are extroverts and some are introverts. Some drive a car, others don't. Some want to be with people, others don't. Therefore, it would be a mistake for professionals to pigeonhole us into a specific category. It just can't be done because we are so diverse.

Part of what we can celebrate about ourselves as individuals with Asperger's is our diversity. Though we have certain characteristics that bind us together, we are also matchless individuals all unique in our own right. Though some of us may be intrigued by railroad schedules, others by game shows, none of us have the exact set of interests as anyone else. Einstein and Wittgenstein, two individuals said to have Asperger-like qualities, were uniquely distinct in their own right. Their interests (science and linguistics) propelled them to be two of the most memorable and important names of the 20th century. Today there are individuals who may not share a lot in common with Wittgenstein or Einstein other than having Asperger-like qualities and being extremely successful in his/her field. Nietzsche may not have had a lot in common with the others, but he also had Asperger-like qualities and he was a great philosopher.

What binds us together as groups in laymen's terms? Our social difficulties. We all experience difficulty with interpersonal interaction, otherwise, we would not have the syndrome. The difficulty we experience is not because we are inferior, or from another planet (as Asperger's is often called "wrong planet syndrome"). It is not because others are better than us, although it is easy to think that. It is not because we are stupid or less intelligent than others. No, it is simply because we are wired differently. We are wired in such a way that we process information perhaps a little slower than others; we are more unidirectional than others. Consequently, attending to the environment at large takes considerable more energy than others. Our social heart beats a lot faster than the neurotypical's social heart.

Indulge me in the concept of a "social heart" for a moment. Imagine that attending a party is equivalent to running a twenty-six mile marathon. A neurotypical's heart beats at the normal rate and gives him or her plenty of stamina to complete the race. We, on the other hand, have a heart that beats slightly faster. Our heart has more work to do than a neurotypical's heart and consequently, tires easier. It doesn't mean our heart is defective, it just works harder. We have to work a little harder at socializing. It comes naturally to many neurotypicals but it doesn't come naturally to us. Our "social heart" works in a slightly unconventional way.

Let's imagine another kind of heart--the "focused heart". Imagine for a moment that a neurotypical is put into an isolated room and given ten books, ten videos and ten DVD's on his or her subject of interest. Suppose he or she was asked to become an expert on this subject without the luxury of being able to collaborate with others. They had to do it all from their solitary room; no social interaction, no peripheral environment to keep track of just themselves and their materials. How focused would they be? Would they become bored easily? Would you?

If there was such a thing as a "focused heart", my estimation is that Aspies on the whole would have a stronger focused heart, while the neurotypicals would have the unconventional "focused heart". Perhaps this kind of "focused heart" is the reason for the success of the Wittgensteins, and the Einsteins. Perhaps without the strength of their "focused hearts", they wouldn't have become the prominent people they are.

Unfortunately the world we live in values the social heart much more than it values the focused heart. Success in the world is often dependent on the strength of one's social heart. Most of the jobs in the workplace require one to have sufficient multitasking abilities, as well as being interpersonally comfortable with others. Let's break it down:

© 2005 Nicolas W. Dubin

1. The social heart loves to multitask and is multidirectional, being able to soak up one's peripheral environment including the five senses with relative ease. For example, the social heart is able to know everything that is going on in a classroom, having "eyes in the back of one's head".
2. The focused heart loves to be "one-dimensional" by nature and has trouble integrating incoming stimuli of the peripheral environment cohesively with the five senses. For example, it can only focus on one element of a situation at a time. "I can only take attendance right now. I'll answer your question when I'm done, Johnny".

The focused heart also loves predictability. Without it the capacity to focus is diminished. If you are totally immersed in what you are doing and all of a sudden someone knocks at the door, what are you going to do? Jump out of your seat! A neurotypical probably would do the same thing. But particularly for us, in order to stay focused and in our element, we need to know exactly what to expect.

The social heart on the other hand, is used to change in the environment and can adapt to it with much less difficulty. It is not as bothered by unpredictability and can adapt to surprises and changes.

The world is filled with unpredictability. Rarely does a day go by that something doesn't go according to plan. When things do not go the way we expect them to, for us Aspies, it can throw us into complete pandemonium. This is another element of living that is tougher for us than neurotypicals!

For example, I recently got a flat tire. Not a very big deal, right? Well, for me it was. It threw me into a state of rage because I was dealing with other events throughout the course of my day that were overwhelming. What were those events? Errands, a therapy session, and meeting my parents for dinner. Why were those events overwhelming? Because they taxed my social heart! For me, they took more energy than the average person. By the time the flat tire incident took place I had very little energy to deal with it rationally.

We cannot avoid these situations in life. Things are going to pop up in our immediate environment that will take our attention away from what we are doing. Changes and surprises will take place during the course of the day. Little things that might not take a lot of energy for most, will take more energy for you. By the time you have to deal with everyday stresses it can put you over the top. We have to accept the fact that in this area of our lives, it is going to generally be more difficult for us than for neurotypicals. But that doesn't mean we cannot learn strategies to help us handle change and unpredictability with greater ease. Perhaps we can stretch the social heart's muscle just a little bit.

As I see it, the main difference between autism and Asperger's Syndrome is the degree of "hyperfocus" a person has. Hyperfocus is a clinical term that is synonymous with "tunnel vision" awareness. An individual diagnosed with low functioning autism may be consumed with his or her momentary focus to the exclusion of the external world. For example, think back to Rain Man. His focus at different points throughout the movie was the television show People's Court, or the K-Mart in Cincinnati. He was so fixated on those subjects that he literally could not attend to the world around him. Obviously, Aspies are not as hyperfocused as other friends on the spectrum. Our hyperfocus is a little more invisible, but it is there. It causes the rigidity in thinking that we are so notoriously known for. Why? Well, here's an example:

Think back to when I asked the girl if she painted her face red. A thought entered my mind when I initially saw the girl; "That girl must have painted her face red." I was so hyperfocused on that particular thought I didn't allow other possibilities to enter my mind as to why her face might be red. The intensity of that thought blocked all other thoughts from entering my mind. This is what I would call "internal hyperfocus". In other words, internal hyperfocus is focusing on a thought. But there is also "external hyperfocusing" too. External hyperfocusing comes into play when a person is asked to do more than one thing at the same time. The demands are coming from the external world, not one's internal world. So the focus is outside of oneself. An Aspie generally can only maintain his/her focus on one thing at a time. We Aspies tend to become fixated on one demand and ignore the rest, which explains our poor multitasking abilities.

My suggestion would be to try to put yourself in situations where you can use your focused heart as much as possible! These are situations where hyperfocusing is actually an asset! This is not to say you should never socialize or be out in the workplace. You should socialize as much as you want to! What I am saying is that your success in life is going to depend on how you're able to channel your creative energies and "focus" them forward, for this is where your strength lies. Find out your talents, your special interests, and immerse yourself in them.

You'll never know how much of an impact you can have in the world unless you try. Just ask Albert Einstein! I strongly believe that individuals with Asperger's Syndrome have many gifts to offer the world. Do you find yourself doubting my words? Do you believe you are capable of making a positive difference? I struggled socially, didn't fit in, and felt like I couldn't make a positive difference. For years these reasons helped me rationalize why I was a useless individual with no purpose or mission in life. I understand more clearly now that sometimes our feelings of isolation can be so intense they block our rational mind from seeing how capable we are of greatness. Figuratively speaking, some see the glass as half empty instead of half full. For the first twenty-five years of my life I saw the glass as half empty.

Aspies are capable of making a difference. Over the past several months I have found message boards on the internet where people with Asperger's Syndrome communicate with one another. As individuals share their thoughts they are expressing themselves in very articulate ways. It's inspiring to see! I have developed new concepts and ideas through reading the message board. I've observed individuals standing firm in their beliefs with honesty and compassion conveyed to others. Those thoughts have made a difference in my life. I thank you for that.

At the same time I know that we are presented with various challenges, and I don't want to minimize these everyday difficulties. Those hidden barriers are so real to us and yet elusive at the same time. With new understanding they will become less elusive, and you will be able to break through some of the hidden barriers standing between you and others.

© 2005 Nicolas W. Dubin

Though I was not raised in a particularly religious environment, I am a spiritual person. Being spiritual, I do not believe that Asperger's is a punishment from the divine. On the contrary, I make a conscious choice to see it as a gift. Let me clarify so there are no misunderstandings:

Although there are things I find difficult about having Asperger's Syndrome, I also think I am blessed in several ways as a result of having Asperger's. I am:

1. An original thinker
2. A very focused individual
3. A nonconformist
4. An intelligent person
5. Compassionate (yes....compassionate)
6. Reflective (introverted)
7. Honest (pathologically so)

Though no two individuals are exactly alike, I believe many of you have these qualities as well. It is my hope that you are able to harness your gifts and channel them creatively to make a positive difference in the world.

I am honored that you have invested time in reading this book. Through sharing my experiences, I hope you have a better understanding of Asperger's Syndrome, and a greater appreciation for individuals-- possibly yourself-- with this diagnosis.

References

Armstrong, Louis. I'll be Glad When You're Dead You Rascal You.

Grandin, Temple. Thinking in Pictures:And Other Reports from My Life with Autism. Random House, 1996.

Newport, Jerry, and Mary Newport. Autism-Asperger's & Sexuality: Puberty & Beyond. Future Horizons, Inc, 2002.

Newport, Jerry. Your Life is Not a Label: A Guide to Living Fully with Austism and Asperger's Syndrome. Future Horizons, Inc, 2001.

Shore, Stephen . Beyond the Wall: Personal Experiences with Autism and Asperger Syndrome. n.d.

Shore, Stephen. Uncommon Places: The Complete Works. Aperture, 2004.

© 2005 Nicolas W. Dubin

Aspie Self-Checklist
Traits Exhibited By Nick Dubin
© 2005 Nicolas Dubin
This checklist was designed as I was assessing what I felt were the Asperger traits that fit me. Have fun as you go through the list.

__X__ 1. I feel incompatible with the culture I was born into. I feel culturally "illiterate," That is, I do not know what movies are currently showing and do not really care. I do not like the current pop music of the day. My musical tastes are different from most people my age.

_____ 2. I often feel that if I cannot be the best at what I attempt, I shouldn't attempt it at all.

_____ 3. Multitasking (or doing many things at the same time) is almost impossible for me.

_____ 4. I crave positions of control and responsibility because I hate being told what to do, but I worry that I do not have the necessary abilities to handle such a job of authority.

_____ 5. Perhaps nothing makes me angrier than seeing injustice.

_____ 6. Separating from my parents was or is a very difficult thing for me.

_____ 7. My childhood went by too quickly. I do not feel ready to tackle the "real world."

__X__ 8. I do not like the idea of drinking alcohol or taking drugs because I want to be in control of my own behavior. I do not like the idea of being controlled by any substance.

_____ 9. I would hate to be hypnotized because the idea of someone controlling my behavior is unacceptable.

_____ 10. I find it difficult to pick up the general theme or plot of most movies I watch.

_____ 11. It takes me a few seconds to process what the other person has said before I can give a meaningful response. This is often frustrating for me because it seems like others can respond much more quickly than I can.

_____ 12. As a child, I had a speech delay that quickly caught up to age appropriate levels.

_____ 13. As a child, I found the activities in school, such as handwriting, art, and physical education very laborious.

_____ 14. In school, I tended to tune out what I was not interested in.

__X__ 15. I received some special education services as a child.

Breaking Through Hidden Barriers

_____16. I attended a university.
_____ 17. I am fascinated with how things change over time.
_____ 18. I usually have a "one track mind."
_____ 19. I often lack "common sense" when it comes to everyday tasks that seem easy for others.
_____ 20. I have a problem "seeing the forest for the trees", or understanding what is important and what is not.
__X__ 21. I have difficulty generalizing information from one experience to another.
_____ 22. Even though I have high standards for people, I often tend to trust too easily.
_____ 23 I am not a rule breaker, regardless of the situation.
_____ 24. I am one of the most ethical moral people I know.
_____ 25. A member of my immediate family has been diagnosed with an Autism Spectrum Disorder.
_____ 26. Authenticity is vitally important to me.
_____ 27. The idea of a menial job where I cannot express my creativity is revolting to me.
_____ 28. I have certain political, world or social views that are well outside the mainstream.
_____ 29. If I'm going to do a job, I get the job done right, although it might be slower than expected.
_____ 30. I cannot start another project until I finish the one I am currently working on.
_____ 31. As a baby, younger child and even today, I was and am especially finicky about certain foods.
_____ 32. I am a perfectionist.
_____ 33. I find dates (calendars) to be fascinating. I like to know when things occurred.
__X__ 34. I am serious most of the time. People have often told me to "lighten up".
_____ 35. After a long day of expending energy, I need lots of downtime.
__X__ 36. I have a temper that can come out at unexpected times.
_____ 37. I need things to be a certain way, and I will literally go into a meltdown state if they are not the way I want them. Relatively small problems throughout the course of a day can send me into a meltdown state. For example, a flat tire, flight delays at the airport, a restaurant being out of a certain food, etc.
_____ 38. I hate transitions throughout the course of a day.

© 2005 Nicolas W. Dubin

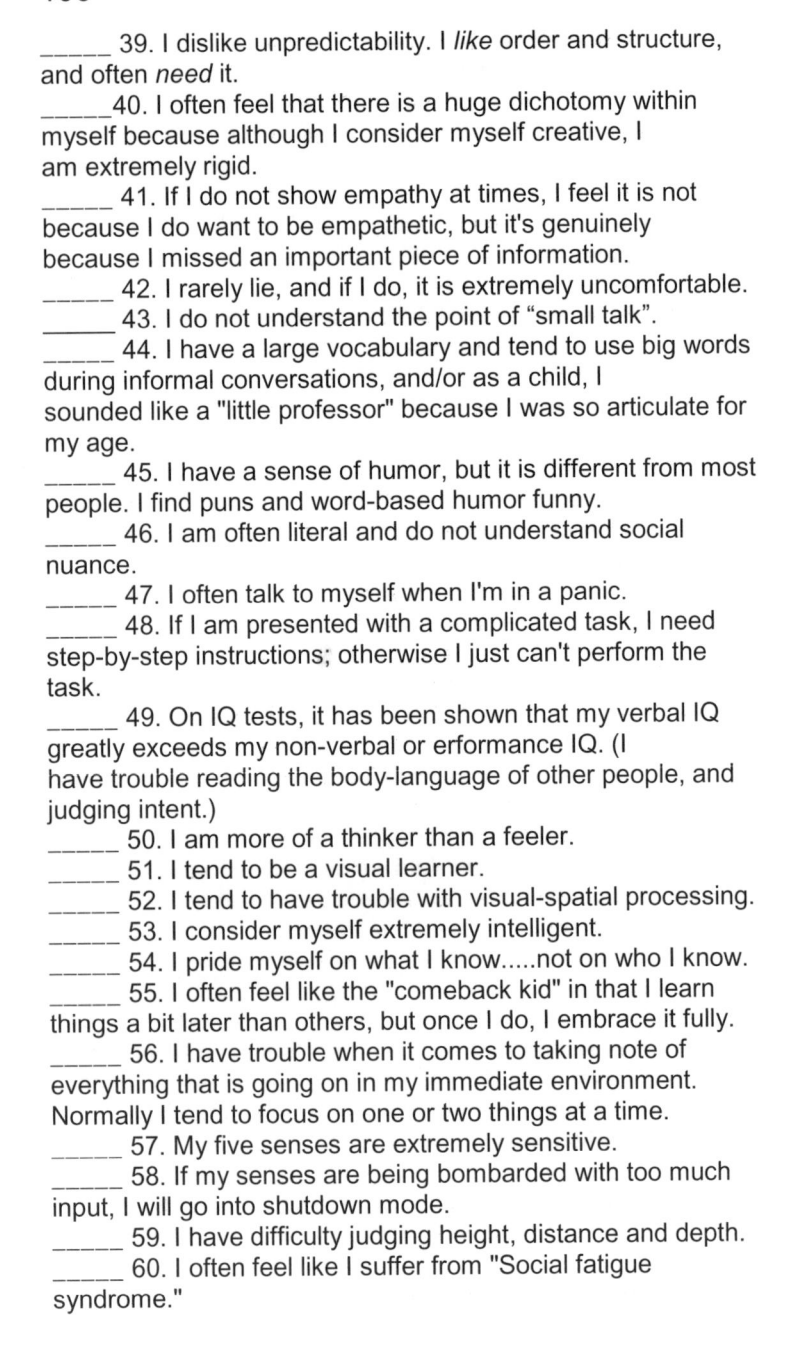

_____ 39. I dislike unpredictability. I *like* order and structure, and often *need* it.

_____ 40. I often feel that there is a huge dichotomy within myself because although I consider myself creative, I am extremely rigid.

_____ 41. If I do not show empathy at times, I feel it is not because I do want to be empathetic, but it's genuinely because I missed an important piece of information.

_____ 42. I rarely lie, and if I do, it is extremely uncomfortable.

_____ 43. I do not understand the point of "small talk".

_____ 44. I have a large vocabulary and tend to use big words during informal conversations, and/or as a child, I sounded like a "little professor" because I was so articulate for my age.

_____ 45. I have a sense of humor, but it is different from most people. I find puns and word-based humor funny.

_____ 46. I am often literal and do not understand social nuance.

_____ 47. I often talk to myself when I'm in a panic.

_____ 48. If I am presented with a complicated task, I need step-by-step instructions; otherwise I just can't perform the task.

_____ 49. On IQ tests, it has been shown that my verbal IQ greatly exceeds my non-verbal or erformance IQ. (I have trouble reading the body-language of other people, and judging intent.)

_____ 50. I am more of a thinker than a feeler.

_____ 51. I tend to be a visual learner.

_____ 52. I tend to have trouble with visual-spatial processing.

_____ 53. I consider myself extremely intelligent.

_____ 54. I pride myself on what I know.....not on who I know.

_____ 55. I often feel like the "comeback kid" in that I learn things a bit later than others, but once I do, I embrace it fully.

_____ 56. I have trouble when it comes to taking note of everything that is going on in my immediate environment. Normally I tend to focus on one or two things at a time.

_____ 57. My five senses are extremely sensitive.

_____ 58. If my senses are being bombarded with too much input, I will go into shutdown mode.

_____ 59. I have difficulty judging height, distance and depth.

_____ 60. I often feel like I suffer from "Social fatigue syndrome."

_____ 61. Socializing is harder and takes more effort for me than academic tasks that interest me.

_____ 62. I often wish there was a textbook on the various pragmatics and the unwritten rules of social interaction because it does not come naturally for me. School was lacking for me in this area.

_____ 63. I identify more with a generation other than my own (i.e. people older or younger than myself).

_____ 64. I tend to be a loner.

_____ 65. Sometimes people tell me that I am "in my own little world."

_____ 66. I strongly dislike competition.

_____ 67. I love helping others.

_____ 68. I love teaching others what I know.

_____ 69. I am extremely loyal to my family.

_____ 70. Having an intimate relationship with another person is something I desire, but I would be worried about losing my autonomy, and having more unpredictability in my life as a result.

_____ 71. I usually have trouble putting a name to a face (or recognizing people).

_____ 72. To me, exchanging pleasantries with people I do not like feels "fake" and is extremely uncomfortable.

_____ 73. I can converse much more fluidly through the Internet than I can face-to-face or over the telephone.

_____ 74. I find most people bizarre and confusing.

_____ 75. I connect easier to animals than to humans.

_____ 76. People could take advantage of me because I am not assertive.

_____ 77. I often found it hard to deal with bullies because I did not have the social skills to eventually befriend them or to defend myself.

_____ 78. I tend to either really like people or hate them. With me, there is no in between.

_____ 79. People have to meet my "integrity standards" before I can decide whether I like them.

_____ 80. I dislike parties.

_____ 81. If someone is going to be my friend, they must meet my standards of honesty, integrity and authenticity.

_____ 82. I do better at individual sports than team sports.

__X__ 83. Sometimes I feel my social difficulties go unrecognized because I have learned to "fake it," at least for a while.

© 2005 Nicolas W. Dubin

_____ 84. Sometimes I have trouble knowing whether someone perceives me as a friend or just an acquaintance.
_____ 85. Sometimes I tend to unconsciously do things in public that are inappropriate: i.e., pick my nose, clean my ear canal, put my coat on backwards without noticing, have on inappropriate clothing attire for an occasion, etc.
_____ 86. Fashion is not exactly important to me.
_____ 87. I do not have great personal hygiene habits.
_____ 88. I always arrive on time to places.
_____ 89. I do not do well with those in authority.
_____ 90. I have fine motor difficulties. Using silverware, writing with a pencil, and doing things that involve use of my hands is extremely challenging for me.
_____ 91. Gross motor skills present great difficulty for me. Throwing a ball and catching it, lifting weights, throwing a shot-put, and other activities that involve larger muscle groups is extremely challenging for me.
_____ 93. I am relatively uncoordinated.
_____ 94. I have an amazing ability to stay focused on tasks or topics of interest for long periods of time.
_____ 95. I hate not being an "expert" in what I am interested in. I equate it with "social incompetence."
_____ 96. I have a collection of some kind............Coin collection, music collection, baseball card collection, collect statistics on a certain subject, etc.
_____ 97. My expertise in areas of interest far outweighs my general knowledge about the world. I sometimes do not keep track of current worldly affairs because all of my time is spent learning more about my special interests.
_____ 98. I either share too much about what interests me, or I share too little.
_____ 99. I rarely read fiction books. I almost always read nonfiction or fact based books.
_____ 100. I have trouble reading the emotions of other people based on their facial expressions.
_____ 101. I have trouble sustaining lasting friendships.
_____ 102. Making jokes and wisecracks does not come naturally to me.
_____ 103. The friends I do have, I am very loyal to.
_____ 104. Understanding the intricacies of subtle humor is something I have difficulty with.
_____ 105. If people do not say what they mean, I cannot read between the lines (or understand exactly what they mean).

© 2005 Nicolas W. Dubin

The Gray Center
for Social Learning and Understanding

4123 Embassy Dr. SE, Kentwood, MI 49546, Ph: 616-954-9747, Fax: 616-954-9749   www.TheGrayCenter.org

The Gray Center for Social Learning and Understanding is a nonprofit 501(c)(3) organization dedicated to promoting social understanding between individuals with autism spectrum disorders (ASD) and those who interact with them in the home, school, workplace, and community.

Success in life is usually dependent on a person's ability to be successful in social interactions with others. "Social interactions," by definition, require more than one person. Therefore, a person with a "social impairment" such as ASD is not the only one who needs to be equipped with skills and understanding to make interactions with others "work." This need is shared by everyone—whether a parent, teacher, sibling, grandparent, therapist, medical doctor, classmate, colleague, school bus driver, pastor, another member of the community, as well as a person with ASD.

The Gray Center is pleased to provide several resources for encouraging and enabling successful interactions. The following is a list of resources developed by The Gray Center. These resources and many others are available on our web site at **www.TheGrayCenter.org**.

Breaking Through Hidden Barriers

The Gray Center's Newest Resources:

- ***Define Me*** (DVD) by Sondra Williams. This two-hour resource contains Sondra's presentation by that title, followed by an interview with Laurel Hoekman, Executive Director of The Gray Center. This is a fabulous way for people to get to "know" Sondra, even if they are unable to meet her in person, or to better understand life from the perspective of a person with ASD.
- ***Reflections of Self***...a book by Sondra Williams detailing her thoughts on being a person with ASD, her childhood memories, her life as a wife and mother, and her faith.
- ***Diagnosis Asperger's: Nick Dubin's Journey of Self-Discovery*** (DVD). This fifty-minute resource provides an informative and sometimes humorous introduction to Asperger's Syndrome through the experiences of Nick Dubin, who was diagnosed with AS at the age of 27. The inclusion of home videos Nick's from childhood are also helpful for parents and professionals working with young children.
- ***Social Thinking Across the Home and School Day*** (DVD and VHS) with Michelle Garcia Winner. This four-hour resource contains practical tips and information for going beyond teaching "social skills" to teaching "social thinking skills" to ensure that individuals with ASD are given the "missing information" involved in social expectations. Following a workshop presentation, Michelle works with children ages 8-13 in groups and individually to demonstrate her instructional techniques.
- ***The Social Stories™ Quarterly***. Containing Social Stories™ and Social Articles™ centered around a quarterly theme of *All About Me, My Home, Success at School,* or *Building Community,* this resource provides a guide for parents and teachers striving to "demystify" social situations for children, young adults, and adults with ASD.

Sondra Williams and **Nick Dubin** are also available to give presentations to school and parent groups and other organizations. For more information about this tremendous resource, e-mail **info@thegraycenter.org**.

© 2005 Nicolas W. Dubin